Preface

Starting to write this story has been a thought of mine for some time. There have been some great mentors and supporters to me along the way. A special thanks to a dear friend who passed away a few years ago Joe Rodwell. Also, an incredibly special thanks to my four children, Chris, Heather, Jeff, and Katie. Each of them has been a true blessing from God. While I may not have been a perfect father at times, they have been perfect children – at least in my eyes. Another incredibly special thanks to my fellow novel genre reader fan, Daniel Singer, who I promised I'd put in my preface.

And for all the men and women who I've worked with in different jobs, locations, adventures, and positions, and who contributed to this novel in a variety of ways and in a variety of areas- "thank you."

Finally, a special mention to Laura Luce Stocker. She has been my support since 1984.

Prologue, or…

How it all Began

April 1981 Colorado Springs, Colorado

He walked into the fast-food joint in search of a fish sandwich. As a good Catholic he still believed in a "no meat Friday", if for no other reason than to keep the Pope pleased and not to end up in an argument with his mother who would be telling him that he would go to hell if he ate meat on Friday.

 The easiest place to find a fish meal on a Friday was fast a food joint for lunch, besides; he needed a place to think about where to find his next recruit. His job as the Recruiter for The Company was to find that special guy or girl who could be at ease with all sorts of people, make friends fast and gain their confidence. It didn't hurt that the person could be trained as a good liar as well, to get themselves out of, or into situations. But the Company could teach him that later.

After getting his tray of fried fish and chips he sat down at a table next to a window. The view of the parking lot was classic. What he saw were the random Old Fords, Chevy's, and the infamous old Pontiac Firebird that someone was in the middle of restoring. He asked himself why is it that no one ever seems to get past the primer paint stage of these restorations. Every one of them you see on the road is always a wreck, looks like crap and is covered in primer grey paint and mixed parts of different colors.

Next to him on his right side were two tables in the middle of the dining room, both had guys sitting by themselves, obviously not knowing each other but dining on the sliders and fries.

The recruiter was not really paying much attention to them at first, but it wasn't long before he noticed the one big guy was opening a conversation with the stranger. Within the first 5 minutes, both guys were laughing and then moving together at the same table to continue talking about everything – yet talking about nothing.

What was becoming of interest to the recruiter was that the big guy, who initiated the conversation, was getting tremendous amounts of information from his newfound friend. Within minutes he knew about his new friends' life, including marital status, number of children, job, which neighborhood he lived in and even into political preferences.

Within 15 minutes you would have thought these two guys were longtime friends and not strangers that had met for the first-time moments ago.

The recruiter listened and noticed the big guy was dressed nicely, spoke well, was obviously educated, and carried himself well.

Could it be he found his next recruit in the dining room of a fast-food joint? Why not?

He waited until the men parted ways and watched as the big guy finished his lunch. Then the recruiter decided it was time to pounce.

He started a generic conversation with the big guy who was unknowingly impressing the recruiter and not aware that he would be one of the next, "associates" of the Company!

November 1981, Colorado Springs, Colorado

Six months after the initial encounter in the fast-food joint, the recruiter had found his new associate for the "company". The new guy had been offered a position within the CIA and had completed a series of training modules over the last six months at the "Farm", back in Langley, Virginia. Now it was time to see what the new associate could do.

His first task was relatively simple. There were a group of field grade army officers in from South America in conjunction with the IMET - International Military Education and Training being held. IMET began in 1976 with the goal to provide a program that provides funding to train military and civilian leaders of foreign countries, primarily at schools and facilities in the U.S.

According to the **Secretary of State**, IMET has three objectives: a) to enhance the capabilities of allied and friendly militaries to participate in peacekeeping operations under the United Nations or other multinational efforts; b) to promote common understanding with U.S. military forces by exposing IMET students to American military doctrine, strategic planning processes, and operational and logistical procedures; and c) to build positive relationships between civilian and military officials from the United States with counterparts in other countries.

This last objective is considered the most important by U.S. officials and this is where the new associate would cut his teeth. His instructions were simple.

Develop a friendship with one of the visiting foreign military Colonels to gain an additional source of information for the Company.

If needed, the associate could inform the "new foreign asset" that a foreign bank account could be set up in their name, and funds would be deposited into the account each month in exchange for accurate intelligence about what was going on in that country.

The new associate turned out to be a natural. Under cover as an educational consultant looking to improve the IMET Classes, he roamed the dining halls and met whoever he was instructed to meet with.

Within the first three months of assignments he had, "turned" seven high ranking officers from South American Countries over to the CIA in cooperation.

His second assignment dealt with The North American Defense Command (NORAD) which is in the Cheyenne Mountain just south of the City of Colorado Springs.

His assignments were to verify the identities of "hostile foreign agents" who were in the area from Russia and China trying to gain intelligence from our own dissident military officers and senior enlisted personnel.

His job was to find out who was trying to do to same thing to our military people, as he was doing to the foreign military personnel. The recruit quickly ascertained and noticed the "covers" of foreign agents are sometimes sloppy and stupid. For instance, they send an Agricultural Expert into the US learning new farm techniques. Certain foreign governments don't fully understand that very few crops grow in the Colorado Springs since the city is at an altitude of 6,000+ feet!? Picking out the foreign spies turned out to be relatively easy.

He did very well in verifying certain foreign agents which resulted in having them deported, but the entire situation constantly reminded him of the old Mad Magazine Cartoon, "Spy vs. Spy". It was the beginning of a long association between the new associate and the Company.

A Beginning-Present Day

My name is Matt Tucker; I saw a blue bird today and I just knew the day was going to be a great one. I've always heard that seeing a blue bird, not a blue jay, is an indication of a great day. The bird flew along with me as I rode my bicycle back to the house from the

A1A, the main beach road that runs parallel to the ocean in Pompano Beach Florida.

The sun had been rising on the waves, with the water reflecting the light like bright diamonds and gold ribbons. The breeze was running through the palm trees making that unique sound you only hear when palm tree branches sway back and forth in the wind.

And of course, the beauty of the beach. I mean, any normal heterosexual guy loves seeing the bathing beauties walking on the sand in the morning.

Yes sir, what great view on the beaches of South Florida in late March! I get to see seventy- and eighty-year-old men and women wearing too little – and showing too much!

It's always the retired guys from the Northeast who get me. Overweight, wearing 20 pounds of gold tone jewelry on their neck, pinky finger rings and gold tone wrists bracelets - topping off their beach look with a black speedo – 2 sizes too small.

And it seems like the "women from Ohio" either wear the brightest Lillie Pulitzer bathing suits ever made or the 2-piece ones from Wal-Mart that remind you of a "handkerchief on a watermelon."

Entering the crushed rock and coral driveway to my house always gives off a nice rustic sound. A much better sound than the whine of tires on a concrete or asphalt driveway.

The sun was out and the soft yellow stucco on my two-story house had a nice Florida feel. The side accents of the house are trimmed in white and the windows in a darker grey. That same color scheme was used to match the large concrete and marble fountain in the middle of the circular driveway out in front.

That fountain had three concrete dolphins spitting water out of their mouth that you saw when you enter the grounds. The pool and guest house are trimmed in the same color scheme.

I mean, come on, everything's got to match, right?

As I approached the house, Winston, my house manager, came out the front door with that look of, "something was needed" on his face.

I hate that look!

"Sir, (I also hate it when he calls me sir) Lt. Hahn called and is on his way over here to talk with you about a situation and he'll be here within a few moments. I tried to reach you on your cell phone but there was no answer – as usual," Winston announced.

He always gets "ticked off" if I don't answer the phone when I take my morning bike ride. What the heck? It's one of the few moments in the day where I get to turn off the electronic world and enjoy the pictures of nature that God put in front of us to enjoy.

Approaching the front door, Winston grabbed my bike, as I heard tires entering the driveway behind me. As I turned around it was Lt. Todd Hahn driving one of those snazzy Grey Ford Crown Victoria's. Why is it, that all the police departments use them? As a detective, why not drive something less, "cop-like". Maybe the police departments should consider a BMW, Mercedes, or Lexus, just anything not so, "obvious cop."

I've helped Hahn and the Pompano Beach Police Department on several cases over the last 5 years as an "Investigator Consultant." I knew a lot of people, they knew me, and besides, I have this God given ability to get a lot of information from people in a noticeably short time.

People always like me. Well almost everyone likes me.

Ex-wives and ex fiancés don't count.

Hahn and I walked through the house out to the pool area and sat under an umbrella with four recliner chairs. Winston was already following with fresh coffee, two small bowls of Greek yogurt with raspberries and bran muffins. For some reason he felt I needed a daily dose of bran and he served it every day to me – as well as any my guests that may be around in the morning.

Winston sat the tray down and walked away when, Hahn when said to me," Matt, you ever get tired of living like this? I mean you're living in a 10,000 square foot house with 6 bedrooms across the street from the beach and it's just the two of you?"

My response to Hahn was in the form of a rhetorical question to him.

"You mean do I dislike living in a mansion on the ocean, with a pool, guest house, tennis court, and my membership to the Atlantic Country Club paid for life plus a Golden Retriever who actually likes me and gets excited to see me when I come home? Trust me, after 2 years I'm getting used to it. And remember, Winston came with the house."

Chapter 1- Two years prior of the present day –

The Bennett's, and Winston

It was late in the afternoon when Arthur and Margret Bennett were finishing getting dressed. It was their 51st wedding anniversary and Arthur wanted to buy his wife something incredibly special at Rossiers, the local fine, expensive jewelry store. They had been married since they were both 18 and still adored each other as much as the day they first fell in love.

Arthur asked Winston to bring the car around to the front of the house. Winston was their House Manager, Butler, and confidant to both Bennett's for the past 43 years. At 68, Winston was still in good shape. While only 6' 4" in height, he had a barrel chest, a full crop of silver hair combed straight back, a well-trimmed salt and pepper beard and a black eye patch covering his right eye.

Side Note: He lost his right eye in an accident protecting his employer, Arthur, from an explosion 23 years ago in Senegal, Africa. Winston single handedly kept a local group of revolutionaries from gaining entrance into the field office of Arthur Bennett's, Bennett International Ltd.

Winston made it clear to everyone, including his employer Arthur that he and the office staff should escape out the back entrance now – not later!

Winston would keep the "bad guys", who were coming from the front of the field office, with his modified 12-gauge shotgun that had a 42-inch barrel used for goose hunting. It had incredible range and accuracy.

In addition to firing his shotgun at the troublemakers, Winston kept a constant blast, of ear-splitting cannon noise and fire spitting from his 50-caliber revolver that had a 9-inch barrel.

In short order, he had the rebels running and hiding behind trees wondering what the hell that noise was coming from.

All Winston heard them yell as they ran and hid for cover screaming was, … "because crazy white man has cannon in house!"

Side notes for you about .50 caliber handguns. The biggest of Smith & Wesson's Magnum cartridges, the .500 S&W Magnum, was the company's successful attempt at recapturing the crown of most powerful production revolver cartridge. Not only did Smith & Wesson seek to create the biggest cartridge in .50 caliber, it pulled out all stops by also making it amongst the highest of pressure producers. Smith & Wesson didn't just want to take the top position back, they wanted to put as much distance as possible between the .500 Smith & Wesson Magnum and its nearest competitor.

As for me, I've used a .50 caliber before. The big .50s require a true dedication to the craft to master, a perishable skill that needs constant upkeep. However, once mastered and loaded properly for the game being pursued, their terminal effectiveness is admirable. I have cleanly taken several large wild pigs with revolvers. The big .50s deliver if the shooter does his/her part.

It allowed the Arthur Bennett's and the other employees to get away safely. Then leaving the area in an open top jeep, Winston took a lucky hit from a stray shot. The bullet passed over the bridge of his nose and right through his right eye. Tough as nails,

Winston kept driving until he met up with the Bennett's at the American Embassy Compound.

Chapter 1a-

Two years prior of the present day –

The Bennett's, Winston and why I'm in this house.

While the Bennett's were extremely well to do and worth hundreds of millions, they are down to earth normal people – always helping someone or something. They did their own grocery shopping (Winston picked up what they forgot) and almost every time they went to the grocery store, Arthur or Margret would slip a $50 bill into the hands of someone who looked like they were counting their pennies while shopping.

Their car was a simple Lincoln Town Car, light silver, the Bennett's (and me included) never could understand why anyone would own a jet-black car in south Florida.

Come on, the sun and temperature alone would regularly bake the interior of a black car to a 125+degrees. You know how it feels to get in and sit on a black leather seat, with a pair of summer shorts on? Ouch, a third degree burn to the back of your upper thigh!

And anyway, most of those people with black colored" high line cars" just wanted to call attention to themselves. Not the Bennett's style.

Unassuming and discreet were part of their lifestyles. They started with nothing, amassed a fortune, and remembered who they were and when they started – and never forgot.

They are a great couple.

Chapter 2

Stay with me.

Rossiers Jewelry was located on Ocean Drive, the nice street with all the exclusive shops in Boca Raton, not more than two blocks from the ocean itself. If you wanted a unique and unusual gift, it could be easily found on Ocean Drive. You're also going to pay a premium for that gift, because everything is unique, custom, and never found or seen – even in the fine department stores like Macys.

There is a small alley on the left side of Rossiers that led to a parking lot in the back of the building for the overflow of cars belonging to shoppers. On the right side of the store is a small frozen yogurt and boutique cupcake store. The shop also advertised nonfat yogurt and gluten free cupcakes.

Both were of interest to Margret, but not to Arthur. At 6'1" and 285 lbs., he still loved the fat in cake and the grains in his bread. Bringing something to him that used Crisco and butter, not margarine was a great way to gain his friendship.

He always joked with the owners of the shop, only when no one else was in the store, that fat free yogurt and gluten free cupcakes tasted like disguised cardboard and Styrofoam.

Luck was with the Winston and the Bennett's today, as a shopper was just pulling away from the parking spot that was located right in front of Rossiers.

As Winston got out of the car, his usual routine was to walk over to the passenger side and let Arthur out first.

This was because Arthur always wanted to assist his wife in getting out of the car by holding her hand. Plus, he had Winston move the front passenger seat up as far it would go so, he had more legroom.

Winston's one good eye caught the two men coming out of the side alley. They were approaching the Bennett's car much quicker than a normal pair of casual walkers would be. Winston knew theses too were too aggressive in their movements and their eye contact towards the Bennet's made him think they were more than panhandlers.

That's when Winston noticed they both had clear latex gloves on and were now covering their faces with pantyhose masks. It was not Halloween!

He knew instantly this was not going to be a good encounter. They came right up as Arthur existed the car, yelling and demanded his wallet, watch, rings, and to Winston, the keys to the car.

Winston looked them both right in the eyes – told them to "take a hike and get a real job."

The taller guy pulled out a midnight special, a cheap 22 caliber and shot Winston twice. One bullet hit his right shoulder and the other shot was lower and hit his upper thigh. Together, the shots caused Winston to lose balance and fall backward onto the ground.

Arthur looked over in rage at his friend in trouble and turned to the shorter guy with a steel look of, "I'm coming for you".

But the shorter guy pulled out an inexpensive replica of a Bowie knife with a 6-inch blade and took a swipe at Arthur.

The knife sliced him on the left side of his chest and cutting though Arthurs yellow polo shirt. Blood immediately was blending into Arthur's shirt when he began another advance towards the perps.

That's when the taller guy, shot Arthur in the face, hitting him in the side of his face and he fell to the sidewalk semi-conscious. Luckily, the shot was off center and only grazed his left temple-but blood was now coming down the side of his face onto his neck.

Seeing her husband, semi-conscience, and bleeding from the knife wound caused Margret to jump out of the car to defend her husband. Not seeing the shorter guy with the knife, he turned it over in his hand, swung hard and hit her square on her jaw with its fake bone grip.

With the rough edges on the plastic knife handle, Margret took a hard hit and had a good slash that started to bleed and run all over her white blouse. Dazed, she fell back onto the car and was now laying semi-conscious on the ground beside their Town Car.

The perps were satisfied that in 30 seconds or less they had done what was needed and began to bend over to pick off the watch, rings, bracelets and the purse from Mr. and Mrs. Bennet.

With everyone out of the car, now they planned to steal the car as well.

Tonight, they'd change the license plates, drop off the car at a "chop shop" tomorrow morning and get a fast $2,000 for the car.

What they didn't see was Matt Tucker coming out of the alley, riding his bicycle, carrying a golf club, it was a pitching wedge, a 10 iron.

Chapter 3 - Present Day Just a little more background

Matt Tucker was a Legacy Member of the Atlantic Country Club where his folks had been one of the founding members. His parents had been killed in a car accident by a drunken driver a couple of years before. And while he enjoyed the club, for him it was a place of serenity while on the golf course. Tucker loved golf and what the game can teach you about patience.

The real value of golf is given to us in the form of patience, practice and seeking advice from other golfers. He wasn't great but probably could've been good with some regular practice. His first love was baseball where he had been a catcher in high school and college.

He prided himself on his golf drives – almost always 295-325 yards – although not always straight! His second shots were not so good.

But his chipping game was excellent, and he could drop a ball 3 feet from a pin at 50-75 yards every time. His putting plain sucked.

The Atlantic Country Club was located on the land behind Rossiers Jewelry Store on Ocean Avenue. From the back door at Rossiers you could see the driving range.

Almost every night after dinner, Tucker would ride his bike up to the range. He lived less than a couple of blocks away and the bike ride was good for keeping his legs and thighs in good shape for the occasional game of tennis. He wasn't any good at that either, but the exercise was a good way to stay somewhat fit.

Tucker figured out that the members were almost always gone from the driving range by 530 pm. The reason was simple?

Most senior members would hurry home, pick up their partner and drive like crazy people, at 40 mph, to get the "Early Bird" price at almost any of the local restaurants. Why they raced to the local restaurants was a mystery because there was generally only a $3 savings per person from the regular prices on the menu after 6:00 pm? Go figure!

If you watched many of the seniors at the restaurants, they always seem to stuff their purses with rolls, sugar packets and anything left on a plate. The other group of seniors, not going out to dinner, headed home for their 5 o'clock vodka/gin and tonic cocktail, or two, or three.

Most of them took their anti-inflammatory, gout, toenail fungus, laxative, high blood pressure or COPD medicine, then had a light dinner and went to bed by 8pm.

Tucker usually rode his blue Schwinn 3 speed bike over to the club with a 10 wedge over the handlebars. It was a great way to relax a bit after his normal working day. Most of the members were pro "wanna be" golfers – who also were convinced they didn't need any lessons. As a result, there was always a huge abundance of golf balls on the right and left side of the driving range to be picked up every morning.

Problem was that none of the grounds staff liked going over there to the sides of the driving range retrieving the hooked and sliced golf balls.

The range balls were mixed in the mud, pine straw, loose sand, fallen palm leaves and the occasional but plentiful harmless garden snakes.

So, most nights Tucker used the time to practice his wedge shots and chip them back onto the main part of the driving range for the club.

The golf staff was appreciative of him for that – and he enjoyed conversations and kidding with the ground staff as well.

Chapter 4. Two Years Before - Okay back to it.

Today, it was a lucky day for the Bennett's!

Matt Tucker decided to come to the bakery store next to Rossiers early, get an iced tea and a red velvet cupcake – with gluten. After he ate the cupcake – or two, and finished his iced tea, he would stop by Rossiers Jewelry for a quick replacement battery for his watch.

Then he would ride behind Rossiers, park his bike against a palm tree and chip in between 100-125 badly hit balls from the members, putting them back onto the driving range. He really loved the short irons and what he could do with them.

Even the pros at the club asked him for advice - always in private - regarding those short iron clubs. He would gladly explain it to the pros for free. But of course, the pros took his "advice" and charged $125 per hour to the members. It was probably another reason the staff always had a tee time for him – whenever he asked.

Tucker loved that 10 iron and what he could do with it.

As Tucker came out of the alley and onto the sidewalk on his bike, in front of Rossiers, it didn't take a rocket scientist to see this was a shitty scene.

Two elderly people, unconscious, bleeding profusely and a third guy by the side of the car in similar shape rolling around in a semi conscience state.

Tucker saw the perps beginning to work on the couple arms and wrist trying to get the jewelry off the Bennet's fingers, hands, and necks.

Matt Tucker hated bullies and always stepped in whether he was wanted or not. This was going to be no exception. He had to act fast and use his wits.

The perps looked up saw him and told him to," get the hell otta here before we give you some of the same."

Not intimidated because of some previous training, Tucker replied," hey jerk face, you know who these people are? They're both big time jewelry designers with no less than $100,000 more jewelry in the trunk. I'll show you how to pop the trunk open".

Completely taken off guard and surprised by Tucker's response, the short guy, Mr. Cheap Ass Knife, told his partner to "get the old farts shit, while I get this load from the trunk."

Greed and stupidity will get you every time.

Tucker quickly walked around to the back of the car and began to pretend to open the trunk lock. He only needed about 2 seconds before the perp looked down at the lock to inspect what was going on. That was just enough time that Tucker needed.

Tucker grabbed the guy's hair and mask from the back of his head and bounced his face down against the trunk. He slammed the guy's head down so hard and fast; it dented the lid and two of his teeth rolled out of his mouth as he hit the pavement. Half conscience, as he looked up trying to hold onto his knife, but

Tucker took a beautiful ¾ swing with his 10 iron and connected with the guy's nose sending him into a painful but deep sleep.

In addition to hearing the crack of the nose cartilage, blood was now coming from the perp's forehead, nose, and mouth. He was out cold.

"Nighty night shithead!" mumbled Tucker.

When the tall guy with the gun heard the boom - not knowing it was his partners face bouncing off the trunk lid, he looked up and away from his efforts of trying to get the diamond watch off Margaret's wrist.

He saw Tucker coming around from the back of the car.

The perp picked up his gun off the ground and began to point it at Tucker.

But Tucker had quickly closed the distance between them coming from the back of the car.

He had the advantage of the fast pace and the element of surprise with him.

Tucker swung the 10 iron like a Louisville Slugger baseball bat and connected dead center on the backside of the perp's right hand.

Not sure what was louder, the crack of the perps four broken fingers or his screaming in pain.

As he looked at Tucker, he began his final charge, only to understand Einstein's Theory of E=mc2. Or put another way, he was nano seconds from feeling the combination of energy and mass from the 10-iron connecting to his jaw.

More teeth littering the sidewalk.

Tucker was hoping he won't get fined for causing litter.

Tucker mumbled a couple of words from the song, "Another one bites the dust-yeah!"

Tucker then made a quick survey of these three people bleeding and semi-conscious.

He knew he couldn't handle helping three seniors all at once and calling 911 was going to take too much time and too much blood was going to be lost by these elderly people.

He remembered that Boca General Hospital was only 2 miles away and at this time of day, there was little traffic on the road. He decided he could load everyone into the Town Car and get to Boca General in 3 minutes or less.

Winston was coming around, so he helped Tucker get Mr. Bennett into the back seat.

Winston was looking real pale and really perspiring so Tucker told him to "get in the back seat with Mr. Bennett and I'll get his wife into the front seat with me". Tucker tenderly, but quickly put Mrs. Bennet into the front seat with him. He walked around the back of the car and picked up the knife, gun and a sorry looking 10 iron with a 90-degree bend in the shaft.

The robbers were out cold littering the sidewalk area.

As two employees came out from Rossiers, Tucker told them, "Dial 911 and don't let this pair of slime get away until the cops get here. Tell them I'm driving this group to Boca General!"

He jumped into the front seat of the Town Car with three bloody seniors, two of which were unconscious, and he was now on his way to Boca General. From the time Tucker came around the alley, mixing it up with the two robbers and loading everyone in the car was only about 3 to 4 minutes. Before Tucker got there, Winston and the Bennett's were already cut, shot and bleeding seriously.

Another side note: There are a couple of nice benefits to owning an American Luxury Car like the Lincoln Town Car with its V-8 engine made in Detroit. They can accelerate very quickly when needed and can easily haul ass.

After gaining speed, and getting onto Federal Boulevard, Tucker also called 911 – gave the operator his name and told her, "There's a robbery in progress and gunshots were fired right now in front of Rossiers Jewelry Store. The robbers were armed, dangerous, stupid and currently unconscious on the sidewalk in front of the store."

He told the 911 operator his name and told her to inform Lt. Hahn as well and that he would be with the injured victims at the emergency room at Boca General if they wanted to come over for more details.

"The perps are going to need some medical attention" was the last set of details Tucker gave the police dispatcher.

As he approached the hospital emergency area and seeing that there were no ambulances or any other traffic in front of the emergency entrance, Tucker pulled into the hospital's ER driveway at 50+ mph. He slammed on the brakes making one heck of a tire squeal while braking, coming to a stop just feet from the front door of the entrance to the emergency room.

In fact, the car stopped so close, that the automatic doors opened when the Lincoln finally came to a stop.

Tucker had intentionally pulled that braking and noise maneuver just to gain the full attention of the medical staff that was on duty. It worked well!

Doctors, nurses, and orderlies all came out and Tucker yelled out to them, "You've got three seniors with gunshot and knife wounds!"

Three gurneys and a whole group of medical staff began working on the Arthur and Margret Bennett and Winston within seconds. Orders being yelled and acknowledged, carts with machines, medical devices, medicines, and drugs appeared magically. Each person had a team working on them with lighting speed and skill that can only be found in a hospital ER.

Matt stayed in the immediate area for what seemed to be forever, watching all the medical staff with their skill at work on the three people that he never knew of or met before tonight.

After about 20 minutes, almost in unison, each medical team gave him the "thumbs up" sign for the three people he had brought in. They were going to make it.

About 15 minutes after that the lead doctor came out and talked with Tucker.

"In this case your instincts were correct. Bringing them here as soon as you did keep them from losing too much blood and having some more serious and complicated long-term issues.

They're going recover simply fine, other than some stiches, and some sore bones. You saved all three of their lives," said Dr. Jackson.

He continued, "I only wish that the creeps that did this would get caught and punished. Looks iike the creeps got away clean!"

Not exactly!

As the doctor finished his remarks, two ambulances came rolling in escorted by two police cruisers that were following and transporting- you know who!

Tucker turned to the ER doctor and said – "they didn't exactly get away clean Doc, here they are!" With that said, in came the two "perp" patients bleeding all over – dazed, confused and hurting, although each one missing some teeth.

Accidents Happen

They had broken noses, dislocated jaws, missing teeth, cut lips, goose eggs on their foreheads, broken fingers, and black eyes. One of the perps also had a broken arm.

That may have "accidently" happened as Tucker drove over him on the way to the hospital!

The other perp had two dislocated kneecaps that also, "accidently" happened when Tucker "mistakenly" put the car in reverse, running over the perps' legs before he drove forward leaving the scene!

After reading their drivers licenses and learning their identities, Tucker made sure the Mr. and Mrs. Bennett's were put together in the same room, with Winston in a room next to theirs. They'd all been given sedatives so they would sleep very well that night.

The medical staff was really concerned about the safekeeping of the jewelry, watches, necklaces, and rings they had taken off the Bennett's in the ER.

Tucker told the staff he had to go move the car and for them to hold the jewelry until he came back. Five minutes later he was back after parking the car and took the bag of jewelry from the staff for safekeeping.

He decided to stay at the hospital and sit in the room all night with the Bennett's just in case one of them woke up wondering where they were, or how they got there and who was okay.

After about 30 minutes of answering the questions for the police and Detective Hahn, Tucker realized he was hungry and had missed dinner. He went down to the hospital cafeteria and decided on two pieces of apple pie and some iced tea.

Apple pie really makes most things better in life– and Tucker loved a good piece of cake or pie.

Around 9:00 o'clock that night, Matt opened Mr. Bennett's cell phone, located their daughter Kathryn in his contact list under, Kathryn-Daughter.

She lived in Philadelphia and Tucker called her and explained what happened to her folks and who he was.

The only problem was that she and her two brothers had taken their annual Bennett's Siblings Weekend, less their wives, husband and children and were in Goose Bay Canada.

He reassured her that her parents and Winston were fine and sleeping well. She probably ought to notify the other brothers or sisters and make plans to come down to be with her parents.

Tucker gave her his cell phone number, the hospital name, contact info and room numbers and suggested she call back in the morning.

She thanked him for helping her folks and for calling her- as well as reassuring her that mom, dad, along with Winston, were in good medical hands, safe and resting well.

It was going to take the Bennett's children a couple of days to get out of Goose Bay area and travel to Florida. Located at Otter Creek in Canada is a seaplane base that also provided airlifts to local communities and tourist lodges in the interior of Labrador.

Around midnight Arthur Bennett woke up momentarily, looked around to room and began to panic.

Tucker leaned over, took his hand, and reassured him that everyone was safe and sound. Then he had Arthur turn to his head left so he could see his Margret sleeping peacefully in the bed next to him.

The bandage on her jaw concerned Arthur, but Tucker told him it looked worse than it was. Seeing her sleeping comforted Arthur. Anticipating Arthurs next questions, Tucker told him, "Winston was also fine and was in the room next door resting just as comfortably."

Tucker joked and said, "After all Mr. Bennett this is a hospital not a mixed college dorm, only married couples in the room". Arthur smiled, rolled over and went back to sleep.

Tucker sat in the chair, turned down the lights in the room and went to sleep.

Chapter 5 Present Day

Lt. Dave Hahn was a 9-year veteran detective of the Boca Police Force. Dave grew up in Kansas, played football in college for an east coast university, and spent 4 years as an undercover Navy Intelligence Officer on loan to the CIA. He was assigned to a unit that investigated drug cartels and their laundering of funds from terrorist organizations. After 10 years of chasing the bad guys, being shot at (hit on four different occasions) and living the "California Lifestyle" it was time to change his geography. He always tells the story that helped him make the final decision to head out of California for a place in America a little more sedate. I love the story and want to share it with you as well!

Hahn told me," I was in a restaurant one day by myself having an executive lunch – steak, potato and a salad – also known as a McDonald's Big Mac, fries and a diet coke. In the booth next to me, I overheard (occupational hazard) two construction guys talking about stopping work early today to get to their appointments at 430pm- for pedicures! They were going "clubbing" tonight, looking for that special woman, and were going to be wearing new sandals. So, they needed their feet and toes to look good. That was it – time for me to move!"

Sitting by the pool and finishing our coffee along with our bran muffins, Hahn got to the subject he came over for.

"Matt, I need some help from you on a case that just came up and was given to me". He continued," We just got a tip that some large amounts of drugs have been coming into your country club as a drop off and transfer point before moving up the East Coast for distribution. We're not sure how its working, but the informant said the operation has been working well for the last month. He told us the shipments are 100 plus kilos of cocaine at a time and increasing in weight with each shipment. In addition, the money for these shipments was being exchanged at the club as well as for future purchases".

Well, I knew there are quite a population of rich old farts that are playing poker with pots around $5,000 to $10,000 ending with some occasional hard feelings, but trying to comprehend 100 kilos of cocaine being handled caused me to think, how it was being done and by which member?

Hahn said," Matt, you're a member of the club and people know you do some work that involves shipping drinking water systems, medical equipment and trucks internationally, so maybe you could keep your eyes and ears open and let me know if you see or hear anything out of the unusual?"

"Sure Lt. Dave., the first time I see some of the ladies from the bridge club doing some white lines in the Card Room, I'll call you", I responded.

Hahn didn't think that was so funny and responded, "Hey smart ass —you're a member, I'm not, the last thing we need to do is to issue a search warrant for drugs at your club, piss off a bunch of well-connected members, give the press a story they can fabricate on the abuse of power from the police department and end up showing our hand to the drug dealers. All they'll do is to move the operation somewhere else. Besides, 100 kilos of blow - and increasing in shipments and weight is some serious shit being moved."

.

"Dave, take it easy, I'll start to look around! By the way have another bran muffin that Winston made, I think your systems plugged up and you need some relief" I replied.

We finished breakfast, talking about each other's social life. Dave was seeing a great attorney in the DA's Office, Susan Stinson, and that seemed to be going well. I was happy for him because he was truly a great guy and had become a good friend of mine. Susan had moved here from Iowa by way of a 5-year stopover in Denver at the States Attorney's Office.

As for me, I had been dating a veterinarian, Connie Faylor for the last year. She is super and I feel lucky to be with her.

Okay - another side note: I met her by accident one day as I found a stray Beagle that was sitting by the side of the road and injured. It was early one morning on my usual bike ride when I came across this dog lying next to a garbage dumpster. It was obvious he was in a lot of pain, so I lifted him up, carried him 2 blocks over to the Vet Clinic that I pass almost every day. The office hadn't opened yet, but I could see someone in there. Banging on the door, Connie Faylor, DVM opened the door, took us in and the rest is history.

In the following week, one of her staff took to liking the Beagle.

Me, I took to liking Connie.

And guess what? Connie took to a liking me!

Chapter 6

After breakfast with Lt. Dave, I began to think about our club and its members. Did I see any real unusual activity going on? Maybe someone was flashing some cash and bought an exotic import. That was a stupid thought; there were more exotic imports at our club than American cars. Maybe someone was wearing some new jewelry. Another stupid thought.

There were more diamonds – fake ones and real ones than a DeBeers Showroom.

How about a new boat or yachts? Maybe, but our serious group of members who owned boats in our club were always trading up to the next larger size.

I'd just have to start asking around.

And who was better to ask than the people that worked at the club.

If you really wanted to know what was going on in the lives of country club members – ask a 19th Hole waiter or waitress.

Or the men's locker room attendant. They hear all – know all.

That's the ironic part about a country club. The members think because of their money and position in life they're better than those who work at the club.

My parents always told me that regardless of a person's job, we're all the same and everyone deserves respect. In fact, most club members treat the staff like they really don't exist.

As a result, they talk freely about having affairs with other men or women, cheating on their taxes, illegal stock tips passed to each other and who's got rotten kids and what they've done lately. They act like no one is listening to them especially when they're being served in the dining room or getting a shower in the locker rooms. Amazing!

I began to write down on paper some names of staff at the club I knew, who would have some juicy news for me. Staff members loved to share the dirt on members who treated them like dirt!

Helen Keller once said..., "All kings have had a slave somewhere in their family. And all slaves have had a king somewhere in their family". I've come to learn that's true.

Chapter 7

After the Bennett's Accident, Two Years Prior

After the Bennett's assault and robbery in front of Rossiers Jewelry, and notifying their daughter and sons, it was about 3 days before the children could get down to Boca. During that time Tucker stayed close to the Bennett's as they began to heal and get their strength back while in the hospital.

Winston recovered more quickly and was released from the hospital after 2 days. He went back to the Bennett's house to make sure all was well.

Tucker learned a lot about the Bennett's and how they started out, just the two of them, and then expanded their business into an international company with offices and employees in 34 countries performing road construction, airport runway work and construction of shipping ports.

Yet in all those conversations, Tucker felt as if he was talking to a very humble man who knew the Good Lord has blessed his business.

They began a friendship based on mutual ideas and beliefs. And both the Bennett's and Tucker believe they had made a new friend in each other.

In fact, on several conversations, Arthur Bennett said he thanked God every day for what he was able to do. All credit was given to God.

How many successful guys think that, much less verbalize it publicly?

Matt learned all about the Bennet's children and grandchildren. They loved their parents but the sad fact was that none of them liked Florida or any part of it, which meant fewer trips to see their parents. Their trips were less frequent with more time in other places like Europe and the Orient. In fact, none of the Bennett's children had seen their folks in over 9 months- and most of them had not been to the Bennett's Florida home in 2 years.

The Mr. and Mrs. Bennett's always happily went north to see their children and grandchildren.

After the Bennett's children finally arrived at the hospital, I excused myself and allowed their family to be with each other. But almost every night for the next week, while they were recovering, and their children had left the hospital for the night, I received a call from either Arthur or Margret Bennet talking to me about their recovery and asking how I was doing.

How was I doing? Heck, I was fine. The only part of me that sustained any damage was my 10 iron that now sported a 90-degree bend in the shaft!

Their children were staying at their parents' house, so it kept Winston busy preparing breakfast lunch and dinners for the Bennett's children. Cleaning the house and doing laundry was a welcomed activity and it kept his mind off the robbery attempt and what else he could have – or should have done.

After about a week, the Bennett's were released from the hospital -
sore, with some bruises, stiches, and a patchwork of bandages, but
otherwise in good condition.

The children all stayed another couple of days and after seeing that
everything was under control, left and went back to their lives up
North.

Strange, how it takes a disaster, accident, or health issue to bring
families together.

I was invited over for festive and warm-hearted dinner the night
before their children left.

It was a grand night with much laughter, with countless stories told
about each other and humorous examples talked about their
personalities, intelligence, looks, in-laws, and jobs.

Around midnight things were winding down and I decided to make
my exit.

It was fun to meet the Bennett's children, and each one of them
invited me to their homes up north. They all tried to compare their
family calendars so their parents could schedule visits as well. I
could easily tell there was no time soon any of them would be
coming back to South Florida. They just didn't like the sun, sand,
and surf of Florida.

They continually referred to South Florida as God's Waiting
Room.

Chapter 7 Present Day

A wedding was being held over at our club - The Atlantic Club. I was enjoying myself along with my "squeeze" Connie. The wedding was for Tobias Underwoods daughter-Stephanie. Tobias was an older obnoxious member who I occasionally gave some golf tips to on using a wedge. Tobias ate too much, had horrible table manners, drank too much, and bragged too much. While he was always cordial enough, I'm sure the motivation behind my invitation to his daughter's wedding and the many other members, was to "show off" his wedding and to ensure additional gifts given to the new bride and groom.

Tobias has made his money via a couple of methods.

First, he had been yachting broker for boats larger than 75 feet in length, and were brought in from the Caribbean, where big shots, professional athletes and movie stars had left them after their fling with boats.

Tobias was in the right place while vacationing in Jamaica when he met his first movie star who wanted to sell her yacht. He offered, she accepted, and he quickly sold it in Ft. Lauderdale to a dentist and from there, his yacht brokerage business took off.

The second way he had "disposable cash" was his wife's trust fund. Turns out she had an uncle who died, no children, and left her 34 million – in cash and securities along with some commercial real estate. While she appeared to know truly little about business – Tobias always acted "on her behalf" – as if it were "his behalf".

And it was a good thing that his wife was a "trust funder" because the economy had recently been tough on yacht sales.

After a couple of dances with Connie, I was thirsty and asked Brenda, our head waitress, if she would get me an iced tea when she got a chance. When she came back to my table, she had a disgusted look on her face.

I asked her if there was a problem and she replied, "not really, but I overheard Mr. Underwood talking about being at the club dock again around midnight tonight!"

"I told him I overheard him talking about being at the dock and asked if he wanted me to stay. He got all pissy and upset, told me to forget that I heard that he was going to be there and go do whatever I needed to do for the reception and stay out of his personal business. Gee, I only offered to help, and the old fart got all up tight and ticked off!!"

I assured her that she did not have to stay until after midnight- but I did decide to ask her if this happened often since she used the word, "again"?

She replied, "He's out there on the dock at least once a week these past months. When we've cleaned up and are ready to leave, and he's out there on the dock fooling around with something in and around the members dock".

She was relieved when I told her she didn't have to stay – but it was making me think back on Lt. Hahn's conversation about drugs coming in and out of the club.

So, I decided I would approach Tobias and strike up a conversation hoping to learn about his late-night activities at the club dock. I asked Connie if she would go over with me and greet our "host" since he was standing by the bar all by himself.

"Tobias, thank you for inviting us to your daughter's wedding. It's been a beautiful wedding and the attention to the reception detail has been fabulous. I'd also like to introduce you to my favorite vet, Dr. Connie Faylor".

Connie is an extremely attractive woman, tall, shapely and a light strawberry blonde. Tobias was beginning to eye Connie from top to bottom, and not in a courteous way. I was sure he was trying to figure out how to get Connie on a yacht for something other than a sale. It was obvious that since he had no animals or pets his interest was more of a carnal nature.

Connie was classically gracious, saw right through his obnoxious and drunk, flirtatious demeanor and lame sexual stares. And after a series of jovial banters back and forth, she excused herself to the lady room. Tobias never knew how close he came to being smacked upside of his tiny head by her!

"You know Tobias; this has been such a perfect evening I almost forgot how much I enjoy sitting on the club dock, looking back at the view of the lights of the club. Maybe after the wedding tonight, Connie and I will just sit on the dock and listen to the water, want to join us?", I said.

His faced seemed to instantaneously change to a concern look and asked,

"Why would you want to waste an evening sitting on our dock, when you could take your personal vet home and have her examine you? It's a Saturday night so live it up, go home, have some great sex with your date and pass on sitting on our club dock tonight!"

Wow –he was really concerned about my sex life, or he didn't want me around the dock latter tonight. Since I had the physical part of my relationship with Connie under control, I had to assume I struck a nerve in his late-night plans.

So, I gently went after the subject again just to see how sensitive he might be.

"You know Tobias; you may be right, but maybe if we sit out there after midnight until 1:30 we could really get in the mood? You know what I mean? Maybe we'll just hang around after everyone's left."

"Tucker don't be a damned fool. That' a stupid idea! Go home after the reception, live it up, but don't waste any of your time hanging around our club dock tonight! Crazy ideas – go home, have fun, but don't waste a perfectly good night by hanging around our dock."

That was it –I knew something was a real concern to him.

So, I backed down with," you know, you may be right, we'll just pass on the dock for tonight – good thinking Tobias, thanks!"

And with that, his face seemed greatly relieved - and I knew where I was going to be around midnight tonight.

The only bad part was that I knew my loving arms were going to be wrapped around a hibiscus tree instead of Connie. Darn.

Chapter 8

Connie and I left the Underwoods wedding reception around 9 o'clock. We drove over to the Red Lion for a nightcap where I explained to her that I had a little surveillance to do tonight.

"Yeah? what's her name, and why would she wait to be your second date of the night, Tucker?" Connie stated with a grin.

Connie knew I sometimes did some late night "work" in addition to my boring real-life career, but I never cheated on anyone and wasn't going to start now. She knew it as well.

After our nightcaps, we took a short drive along the beach, smelled the ocean air and I dropped her off at her condo.

Her condo has a great location, right on the Intercostal Waterway in Pompano Beach. A small older, 2 story complex that had a single tennis court, and a small kidney shaped swimming pool that is located right across the street from the ocean. Her 3-bedroom 2 bath unit is on the first floor, spacious and beautifully decorated in a French Provencal motif.

It seemed like everyone else who came to Florida wanted a part time residence in one of the huge, 30 story plus buildings. All equipped with fitness centers (which hardly anyone used), coffee shops and underground parking, nosy doormen and too many "smells" from lousy retired cooks.

Connie's place was nice, quaint, and homey.

"I'll pick you up around noon tomorrow and we'll head to the beach and an early dinner, okay?"

She smiled, gave me great goodnight kiss, (which lingered in my mind for the next 45 minutes) and said, "be careful, you owe me a real dinner Tucker, this free reception food thing at a club members wedding reception doesn't count!".

After getting back home, I changed clothes, said good night to Winston and headed back to the club. I decided to ride my bike so it could be hidden in the bushes and no one would hear a car or see some vehicle in the parking lot.

I got to the club about 11:45 and looked around to see if there was any activity or cars already there. The clubs parking lot was empty, so I carefully put my bike up against a wall and walked next to the tall row of hibiscus bushes bordering the wall, heading in the direction of the docks, so I could get a closer look at the dock area.

About 20 yards away from the dock there was a combination of tall bushes and a small storage shed used to store some tools and cleaning supplies.

I squatted down and was replaying Connie's goodnight kiss, thinking I probably should have taken Tobias' initial advice. Heck, I could have been at Connie's with her in my arms, instead of sitting in a bug infested shed and the bushes, waiting on a hunch.

After about 20 minutes I heard a car and saw the reflection of the headlights bounce around the parking lot. Then I heard someone walking towards the dock from the parking lot. He was mumbling something to himself under his breath. Focusing on I could see it was Tobias Underwood.

Okay jerkface – why are you here – I thought.

As he approached the dock, he pulled a small flashlight from his pocket and waved it around as if to be signaling someone or something.

Almost immediately, a boat 50 yards offshore that had been unseen or unheard by me, cranked up its engine, turned on its cruising lights and began approached the dock.

Another side note for you.

Our club dock originally was built on the ocean. But tides, hurricanes, bad weather and the lack of boating skills, caused our club to build a small artificial jetty. This way club members could come in from the ocean and go through a rock wall gateway entrance to the dock.

This gave protection from the ocean and allowed them to navigate their boats into calm water, regardless of tides or weather conditions. Since we had agreements with a few other clubs, we allowed their members to come and visit in their boats as well.

As the mysterious boat swung around the end of the jetty and into the dock area, Tobias was shuffling back and forth in a very anxious manner. He was looking over his shoulder to make sure no one else was here or saw him and the approaching boat.

The boat docked. It was a smaller cabin cruiser model that was about 35-40 feet. The boat was nothing fancy, nothing high speed, but rather a classic older Chris Craft Style yacht. I couldn't make out the boats name, but I could see it was flying a Jamaican Flag.

Tobias quickly tied off the lines connecting the boat to the dock 'and climbed aboard. The engine was shut down and then the running lights were turned off. A few cabin lights remained on, but the curtains covered up the brightness as well as any views into the cabin.

Tobias had been helped aboard by a single person. For the next hour, the boat was silent and there were no signs of activity on deck.

Then around 130 in the morning, the boat fired up its engine and the running lights were turned on.

Tobias got off the boat with a small suitcase, untied the lines and stood on the dock as the boat made its way through the jetty and into the ocean. When the boat was out of sight, Tobias walked quickly over to his car. He opened the trunk and threw the suitcase into it. He got into the car, looked around to see if anyone was here, wiped his brow with a handkerchief, started the engine, adjusted his glasses, and drove away.

Okay, well that's not exactly normal yacht broker business hours. But what had just happened?

I was guessing that an exchange of a large amount of cash or drugs had just taken place.

Why had it taken so long? An hour? What had taken place aboard the boat? More planning, more negotiating? But I had been too far away to see or hear any real details, so I was still in the dark – physically and mentally.

It was time to go home and decide about what to think about for the rest of the night.

So, I had a choice of subjects to ponder. The first thought was to consider the events that had just taken place with Tobias and the strange boat rendezvous– or take time to remember that goodnight kiss from Connie that was still on my mind from earlier in the evening.

I decided to drift into blissful sleep thinking about the kiss and I would worry about the events that had taken place with Tobias tomorrow.

Chapter 9

About 830 the next morning, after my evening in the bushes spying on Tobias, Lt. Dave Hahn called me about and asked if he could come over right away. I told him sure, come on over because I wanted to share something with him, I witnessed last night.

Winston already knew that Hahn was coming over so extra coffee and Danish (with bran) were prepared with some fresh fruit and the placemats were set under the umbrella awning by the pool.

Hahn got to my place about 9 o'clock and seemed agitated about something. While we were walking through the house to the pool area, he asked me, "Do you know many of the staff at your club very well?"

Dave knew I treated the staff very well, not like some of the members who thought the club staff were their personal slaves. I always tried to ask staff about their families, hobbies outside work, or their general well-being. They're people just like us. At least that's my philosophy.

Take the time to be nice and show a genuine interest in their lives and be cordial to the staff that serves us. No one is better than someone else.

Some club members have told me I was, "too friendly" and there was no need to engage them like they were friends. "Tucker, they're just "worker bees"!

My response to those members was usually subtle and diplomatic. Usually on the order of, "Screw you! These are good hard-working people who take a lot of unnecessary shit from members."

Hahn started talking before we even sat down.

"Matt, I wanted to come over based on our last conversation about the purported drugs and money at your club. Now I got a dead employee from your club. She was found this morning about 6 o'clock. When the golf course staff showed up to mow the greens, they found her in the equipment shed behind the pro shop". Not letting me ask a question he continued sharing the facts. "She was shot behind the head, base of the skull at point blank range with a .22.

No shell casings, no footprints, nothing! The medical examiner put the time of death around 1030 last night."

I knew from personal experience the advantage of such a small caliber. I'd been trained on its years ago when I was doing some work for one of our government agencies. The .22 LR is deadly at point blank and close range. The .22 is always known for being a "hitman" caliber weapon because the bullet has enough energy to penetrate the skull on the entry wound, but not enough energy to exit, thereby just scrambling up the brain a little bit. So, I knew it can certainly do a great deal of damage at point blank range.

"Who was it?" I asked.

"From what I've learned from other staff, she was an older waitress. Brenda Jorgenson. Did you know her very well?"

The look on my face answered Dave's question before I could confirm I knew her.

"Yeah, she was a real sweetie a hard worker and kept to herself. In fact, she's one of the reasons I wanted to talk to you".

Dave leaned forward with a pensive look on his face.

"Do you know something about this?" He asked.

Being a little shaken at this news I replied, "Yes. I was at the wedding reception for a member last night – Tobias Underwood's daughter got married. During the reception, Brenda told me she overheard Tobias talk about being at the dock late. She asked if he needed any help and he got all bent out of shape and gave her a verbal tongue lashing."

I told Dave about the rest of the events of last night, including seeing Tobias at the dock from midnight until 1:30 am, and the briefcase he brought off the boat.

"Think he had anything to do with this?" Dave asked.

"Not sure, but I do know he didn't want anybody near that dock last night" I replied.

" In fact, he got pretty agitated at me when I quizzed him about it as well. I wanted to see why he got so upset at Brenda when she offered to stay if he was going to be at the club dock late".

"I think I should bring him in for questioning, Matt. This is beginning to look like he could be involved. He's upset at her for offering to help him late at night, you see him get on and off a boat with a suitcase – presumed to be cash or drugs, and a waitress who got on his bad side the same night turns up murdered – execution style", said Dave.

"Dave", I said, "hold off for now. If he did kill her, he's thinks he may have gotten away with it and he's not going to run. But if you bring him in, others that may be involved with him will back off and go elsewhere. Let me talk to him at the club and see what his reaction to her murder is?"

"Okay, but keep me in the loop Matt. The murder of a waitress at a Country Club sells a lot of newspapers and the reporters are going to be asking some tough questions."

We finished breakfast, caught up on each other's social lives, talked some baseball and promised to keep each other informed on any new developments.

As Dave drove out of the driveway, my thoughts went back to Brenda.

Nice older lady, hardworking, honest and a genuine individual.

Who would want to execute her, and why?

Chapter 10

Since I had a standing date with Connie for a day at the beach and dinner, I wanted to call her and tell her the news of Brenda's murder. She was shocked and taken back as we had just seen her the night before. I told her I needed to go talk with Tobias and see his reaction.

Then I would pick her up for our date.

Since it was Sunday, the club had a standing buffet that ran from 10:00 am until 2:00 in the afternoon. While I had no idea if Tobias and his wife would go to the club, I decided to head over around noon and see if he showed up for a meal. Certainly, someone who had just murdered someone would not be too hungry.

Sure enough, Tobias was there alone at a table with enough food on his plate to feed three people. His wife Linda was in a conversation with another member two tables away.

"Morning Tobias, it really was a nice reception you put on for your daughter last night", I said.

Before I could start any type of questioning, he asked me if I heard the news.

"What news", I said.

"That old lady waitress, Barbara, was killed last night and they found her in the storage shed by the dock this morning! How strange, she was just serving us dinner last night," he said.

"Tobias, yes I heard and by the way, her name was Brenda. She was a genuinely nice lady who worked hard for our members comfort." I spoke.

"Well, whatever her name was, but that type of thing isn't good PR for our club is it, Matt?

Bad press and now the other clubs will kid us about it. Not good for recruiting new members. How do you explain old lady waitresses getting killed on club grounds"?

The remark was so insensitive I found myself trying to restrain from grabbing his head and planting his face into his monster plate of eggs, hash browns and poached salmon.

"A nice lady gets murdered on our grounds and all you can think about is the possibility of some bad press and idiotic remarks made by other club members? Are you that insensitive?"

"Matt, I'm sorry she was killed, but she was just a waitress here. Those type people always seem to have problems in their lives", he said.

He was not the least bit upset at her death and showed no signs of being nervous at the discussion or trying to hide the fact he had seen her last night.

He just didn't care. He just didn't seem interested at all.

But I cared! And I knew I had to get away from Tobias and his "better than thou" attitude or there was going to be a bad scene in the dining room.

"Tobias, you really need to be more concerned about people" I said.

"Hey Matt, when Filstrom and I were talking about it earlier, we both agreed it was a shame to lose a worker-bee, help is hard to find", he said.

"Rodney Filstrom and you were talking about this?"

"Yeah, you think my attitude is bad, Filstrom said she was an old bitty who gossiped too much and listened in on too many conversations for his comfort!" He continued, "His remark was one less old lady who was a gossip and a busy-body".

Maybe I needed to talk to Rodney Filstrom?

Looking around the dining room I didn't see Filstrom. Darn. Going over to the reservations desk I asked the hostess on duty if the Filstrom' s was here earlier, or if they had a reservation for later.

"Actually, Mr. Filstrom called and cancelled his reservation a little while ago. Said he wasn't feeling good, and they would not be coming in today" the hostess stated.

Well, I knew where Rodney Filstrom would be on Monday afternoon.

So, I decided to go get Connie, and have our day at the beach. Two bikes had been put on hold as a surprise outing and I was looking forward to a nice bike ride along the beach with my best gal.

When we met, Connie was not surprised at the remarks from Tobias regarding Brenda's death. She had already had her "encounter" with him and knew him to be a "creeper".

Connie asked me, "Matt, doesn't that seem strange that someone would describe her as a gossip who listened in on conversations, a little strange? Especially on the day of her death?"

She was right and it caused me to think more about Filstrom and his remark.

Connie was pleasantly surprised at my "advanced date planning" for a change. We rode bikes about 5 miles south, turned around and came back, all in about 2 hours.

We mixed the bike ride with a couple of stops for ocean sightseeing, some water and using our cell phone cameras for a couple of "selfies".

After the bike ride, we took a quick swim in the ocean to cool off and then an hour resting on the beach blankets. It made for a perfect day.

Winston usually took Sunday off. He enjoyed going over to the Pier and would sit fishing for a couple of hours.

I think he enjoyed the time off to look out over the ocean and reminisce about time gone by. If he caught something, he'd clean the fish on the spot, filet it and offer it to someone whose luck wasn't so good with the rod and reel that day. After fishing, he'd go spend some time at the local casino where he enjoyed time at the Crabs Table. He'd played craps all over the world and was usually on the winners' side each time he went. He'd leave when he was a couple of hundred bucks ahead of the casino. He knew when to leave a crap table -he knew how to play.

Connie and I decided to go back to my place, take a swim in the pool and get the salt water off. Cassidy, my golden retriever jumped in with us and swam around chasing a tennis ball.

Cassidy loved the water, especially if people where in the pool. I had trained her on which end of the pool to swim over to, and where the steps were, so she always knew how to get out of the pool.

Connie and I took a long "exploration" shower together, which is/was always fun, put on some clean clothes she'd brought along, and I fixed some dinner for us.

We both decided on something light, so I fixed a spinach quiche with a small dinner salad and a mixture of fresh fruit that was in the refrigerator and a nice glass of Merlot.

I passed on bran muffins or rolls.

We took our plates out to the pool, solved world hunger issues, and laughed about our day.

We'd just finished dinner when Connie's phone rang. It was an emergency. An owner's dog had eaten some small plastic toys that had been handed to the dog by their toddler in a highchair, that were covered in baby food-applesauce.

"Matt, I gotta go! It's my practice and I volunteered to take the weekend emergency calls.

I'll call you later and if it's not too late I'll come back, and we'll finish that bottle of wine together?"

Connie gave me one of those fantastic good-bye kisses that tend to linger. She had a way with that kiss. One hand around my neck and her other hand going up and down my spine.

Plus, I got some tongue! Stupid toddler in the highchair!

Chapter 11 Two Years Prior – about the Bennet's House

About six months after the Bennett's attack, I received a phone call from Margaret Bennett asking if I would come for dinner on Saturday night. She told me it was going to be an incredibly special occasion.

They were doing very well since the attack. Margret was playing tennis again, twice a week and walking every day. Arthur was playing golf once a week, tennis once a week with Margaret and he was spending time on his treadmill every day. Winston had also fully recovered and spent his time using his weights and dumbbells.

When I arrived for dinner, I was pleasantly surprised to see all the Bennett's children were there as well. They warmly greeted me as we all caught up on our lives and activities in the last six months. After a while I noticed no grandchildren which, at the time I thought was odd but kept the thought to myself.

A fabulous dinner with lively conversation was served in the main dining room followed by desert in the living room. I love desert. Don't need it – but love it.

As we finished desert, Arthur stood up from his brown leather wingback dining room chair and took hold of a plain manila folder that was sitting on the grand piano next to Margaret.

"Matt, we all asked you here tonight for a very special reason".

I was totally dumbfounded. I had no idea why I was there.

He continued," Matt, this document we're giving you, has been signed by Margaret and me. And while it's not necessary but equally important, there's an addendum attached to it, signed by each of our children as well as Winston."

He handed the document over to me to read, while the entire family was watching me, with smiles on their face. Whatever was this about? I had no idea.

The document was titled, "<u>DEED OF TRANSFER</u>".

It clearly stated that the Bennet's house we were in, the house we were celebrating, was being transferred to me!

This gorgeous mansion was being given to me. In addition, there was an account that had been created to pay all real estate taxes and utilities.

When I got through reading the first sentence of the Deed, I looked up and saw both Margaret and Arthur together holding hands and their children standing looking at me with warm smiles. They all started to clap their hands.

"I can't accept this gift – you have children, and grandchildren that are family and who are deserving of this, not me," I said.

Harold, Arthur's oldest began," Matt, when mom and dad first brought this up with us, we all agreed this should happen. You know that none of us really enjoy Florida. Take this with our warm wishes and good thoughts."

Margaret interrupted," Arthur and I have purchased a home in Chevy Chase where we'll be much closer to the children and we're excited about being involved with our children and our grandchildren."

"Matt", Arthur stated," Most of our friends are either dead or in assisted living. We thank God each day we have our health. But the time has come. We don't need the space, and we don't throw the parties we used to – besides no one is well enough to come!" Everyone laughed.

"Besides" said Peggy, the Bennett's oldest daughter, "It's time we get mom and dad to ourselves on a regular basis. It's our turn to be there for them. And the grandchildren are thrilled that their grandparents will be so close and be involved in their activities".

I really did try to state my objection, but the tears in my eyes and being totally chocked up prevented me from stating my objection.

"By the way, after taking care of us for over forty years, we've told Winston he needs to take care of you", said Arthur. "He supervised the management of this house for over twenty years but it's time that he no longer worries about Margaret or me any longer.

That job now becomes the responsibility of our children. Winston will always be provided for by Margaret and me".

Winston and I had become friends over the last six months, and I appreciated his dedication and love for the Bennett's. But I was concerned how he would accept me as his new employer.

No sooner had that thought crossed my mind when Winston walked into the living room. He carried a small silver serving tray with three small crystal shot glasses and a small decanter. He turned to me first and offered a glass, then to Margaret and finally to Arthur. I thought the order in which he was serving was a little strange. Certainly, Mr. and Mrs. Bennet should have been served first.

He reached for the decanter and poured what turned out to be a small amount of a single malt scotch into my glass, then Margaret's, then Arthurs.

When Winston was finished, he proudly stated," Mr. Tucker, it is my great pleasure to offer you my services and my loyalty to you, as my employer from this day forward."

With that the three of us accepted his toast and the Bennett's children all clapped again and came forward wishing me congratulations.

In the weeks following, each of the Bennett's children wrote me a letter stating that they knew of no one they would rather have the estate. They all shared how excited they were that their parents would be so close to them and now to be so involved in their lives and the lives of their children.

They loved the Mid-Atlantic region and faraway places.

Florida was just not of interest to any of them. I felt much better that I had not accepted a gift or had taken something away from them.

Later that night, Arthur took me aside in the study and shared with me what he and Margret had done for their children and grandchildren. Stocks, bonds, and cash had been set aside for the education of each grandchild and a little more for them after they reached age thirty.

Each of their own children had received a very sizeable combination of stocks, bonds, cash, and interest in some commercial buildings located around the country. An additional inheritance would be given to them when the Bennett's each passed away.

I hoped that would be an awfully long time from now.

The Bennett's also had established for Winston, a generous retirement program, over a million dollars in cash, and some real estate. His salary would continue until he died or was no longer able to serve. He could quit working for me anytime he wanted with no penalty – no questions.

I was hoping he'd be with me for a long time as well.

Chapter 12

On Mondays, the Club is closed. But I knew that Rodney Filstrom and some others would be in the men's locker room playing poker. There was a group of seven to eight members that played regularly. Hands were mostly a couple of hundred dollars, but a guy could easily end up losing a couple of grand on a Monday. And yes, there were always some hard feelings for a couple of days.

Rodney Filstrom was a dick. A pretty boy spoiled rotten. His father, Rod Filstrom had been a long-haul trucker from Houston to Alaska transporting oil field equipment and pipeline supplies. Business was good and his dad expanded from two trucks to a fleet of two hundred.

In addition, he started an International Truck Dealership that grew from a single location to over twenty-five locations around the country.

Both the trucking company and the dealerships were called Filstrom' s.

After a heart attack and a stroke, eight years ago, he transferred ownership of the business to his son Rodney.

The first thing Rodney did was to spend over a million dollars to change the name from "Filstrom's", to "Rodney Filstroms"!

He changed the stationery, the dealership signage, truck lettering, all done as if to identify "Rodney the Dick", as the founder.

In fact, he was the "flounder". Thank goodness his father sensed it and limited some of the major decisions to a trusted long-term group of employees.

Rodney lost money almost every Monday. He bragged that he'd just write it off as an Entertainment Expense and that the guys were lucky, they made money off him. His attitude was he was doing them a favor. What a jerk!

As I approached him, I could sense he'd had a few drinks. He was a little unstable and was having a difficult time walking a straight line.

I goaded him a little with, "Hey Rodney, how did you do at the game?', knowing full well the little shit head lost a bundle again.

"Hey Tucker, how come you never play?"

"Cause I'm lousy at cards Rodney and I don't like to lose money", I said.

"Yeah, well a real man would play cards with us Tucker" he said." I lose more money than any of these waiters and waitresses make in a week". "Maybe if they paid more attention to serving us members, and less time listening in our conversations, they'd do better in tips".

"Well, I was really sorry to hear about Brenda", I said.

"Yeah, well she was an old bitty with a big mouth who ended up the way she deserved", he slurred! "These people have got to learn, we are the masters, and they are the slaves. Stay out of our business or pay the consequences. You know what I mean?" Filstrom pronounced.

"Filstrom, you're a piece of work", I started. "They work hard for us and deserve our respect and a little show of gratitude".

"Bull crap, they're all failures in life and this is all they can do and have. They better be grateful for these jobs. And they better stay out of our business. We're trying to make more money all the time and they're jealous of us", he said.

"Filstrom, I don't think anyone of them is trying to get into the trucking business."

"Yeah, well they like to listen in on our other activities and the other parts of our lives they got no business listening to", he said.

His attitude was that of a classic spoiled shithead. But there was something in his eyes that spoke of more than he had just said.

Could he have done it? Could he have killed Brenda? But why? What motivation did he have to commit a murder?

Nevertheless, I had a thought come to mind and I wanted to check something out with Lt. Hahn as I left Rodney slumped in a chair over in the back of the men's locker room.

Chapter 13

After the conversation with Filstrom, I left the club and drove over to police headquarters. I had called Todd on the way to make sure he'd be there and told him I had a favor to ask as well.

When I got to police headquarters, I had the same irritation as always.

The entire first row of parking spaces is marked." Handicapped", and the second row is marked, "Officers", while the third row is for "Visitors?

It's the same thing when you go to one of those huge, big box hardware stores. The first two rows of parking spaces are all marked "Handicapped". And quite honestly, I never see more than one or two of them that have cars in the parking spots.

Do that many people with Handicapped stickers come to the hardware store to buy lumber and bags of cement to do home improvement projects?

Do that many people with Handicapped tags come to the police station?

"Todd, I wanted to check something out in reference to the killing of that waitress, Brenda."

"Why is it every time I do you a favor, sooner or later I end up in the chief's office and he reads me the riot act Matt? You realize the police department is not your personal source of information – right?"

"Yeah, I know, but someone has to help this group of misfits in your office to solve crimes" I stated.

"Well, your murder will probably go unsolved. What do you want?"

"I want to know if someone in particular has registered a 22-caliber handgun with the police" I asked.

"Who is it" Todd asked?

Chapter 14

It was about 1:00 am when the twin engine airplane started to approach the Atlantic Country Club from a northeast angle. The approach the plane was taking was from way out in the ocean and both the starboard and port side lights on the wing were turned on and could now be seen from the Clubs dock from about 5 miles away. It was obvious the plane was descending as it got closer to the ocean's horizon.

About a mile from the Club, the plane made a gradual turn to the left and made a heading south, parallel to the beach and Club. Still descending, the plane reduced its speed, made a sweeping 360 degree turn and returned to its southerly course about 200 feet above the ocean.

A lone figure sitting next to the pilot opened the cabin door and began to throw out three containers, each about the size of a five-gallon paint bucket. He wrestled with the wind and the weight of the containers as he threw them out the door of the plane. All the containers were sealed and each of them had a five-foot line and floating buoy attached.

As the five containers fell from the sky, they dropped quickly to the ocean where only the faint sound of a splash of water could be heard as they hit the water. Each container submerged about three feet under water before it began to rise because of the attached buoy.

Within seconds, the buoy's appeared, still rigidly attached to their containers. Then a water activated green light that was attached to each of the buoys began to flash as they floated in the ocean inches above the waterline.

The sound of the plane's engines became faint as the pilot headed sound and then westward over land as it faded into the sky towards the Everglades.

From the Clubs dock, a lone figure watched as the aircraft approached and then dropped its cargo. He sat in his boats captain's chair smoking a pipe as he sipped coffee from a small cup as the thermos rested on the console. Slowly he poured out the coffee into the ocean, replaced the lid onto the thermos bottle and reached for his night vison binoculars.

He used these binoculars on a regular basis as they had a powerful infrared illumination that is invisible to human and animal eyesight. These babies amplified ambient light 500x!

They were perfect for nautical use or for search and rescue operations. In this case he was using them for the search and rescue of five floating containers in the ocean, just offshore from the Club dock.

Chapter 15

As the man in the boat at the dock started his engines, he remarked to himself, "What a fantastic offshore boat! It is a real pleasure to drive, predictable in its handling, solid as a rock in all directions to the sea. Also, it's nicely done ergonomically at the wheel and far superior to the competition…. What a great boat-well done!"

He was at the helm of a popular fishing boat, a Grady White Freedom 28 foot with a dual console. His boat had 600 hp powered by twin Yamaha 4 stroke twins with counter rotating propellers. At 4000 rpm the boat would easily cruise at 36 mph. Not tonight, that would be way too slow for what he needed to do.

Tonight, with the lights shining down on the ocean from a half moon, no clouds in the sky, calm sea, and some flashing green lights on the buoys, he lit up the engines. He moved the throttle to 6000 rpm, causing the craft to speed up to 55 mph. The bow rose about 30 degrees before it settled back down but he knew he had to cover about 2 miles to the rendezvous sight of the containers and decided to do it as quick as possible.

With his left hand on the wheel and right hand holding the night visions, he spotted the floating cargo. Setting his night vision down on the console, he reached for the throttle and pulled it back slowly, keeping the line to the floating cargo on a straight course.

Backing off to about 1000 rpms he had slowed down to about 6 mph, still too fast for an ocean recovery knowing the weight of the containers, so he pushed the throttle into the neutral position. With the night visions secured in his left hand he spotted the first three containers and with his right hand steered the drifting boat alongside.

When he was about five yards away, he reached for the 8-foot grappling pole with a hook and snagged the first container. Hooking the buoy line and dragging the first container on board, he quickly turned off the green flashing light attached to the buoy. Then he quickly unscrewed the top of the container and felt the contents inside for any signs of water that may have leaked in. As he wiped his hand along the side, feeling no water, he immediately secured the top to the container. Then he placed the container on a flat scale and wrote down the weight – 7 kilos. He knew that current market prices were netting about $2,000 per kilo which made each of the container's worth about $200,000 each. He began his search and rescue for the other four containers.

Locating the other four containers in the area and pulling them on board and inspecting and weighing each container took about fifteen more minutes.

After the last container was on board, he wiped off a combination of saltwater spray and seat from his face. Sitting in his captain's chair, he reaches for his pipe, refilled it with a nice aromatic blend, lit it, took a few puffs to make sure it was lit and poured a cup of coffee from the thermos.

Reaching under the console, he took out a small airline sized bottle of Jack Daniels, poured it into the coffee cup and sipped slowly as he starred out onto the ocean with its silver-colored waves that were starring back at him.

As the boat gently swayed back and forth, and the water gently lapped the boat, he calculated, he was transporting a million dollars' worth of cocaine in the dark of night. He would be paid his regular fee of $25,000 for his services.

The first half of his task had been completed - The recovery. Now the second part of his job began - The transporting.

He had to get the containers down to Fort Lauderdale and into a small marina where a rented van would be waiting for him.

Finishing his pipe and Jacked coffee, he lifted three small travel packs from the deck and unzipped each pack. Each Travel Pack featured a bearing drive spinning reel with drag attached to a rod that was a 7' medium action. All the gear came out of a rugged heavy grade nylon form-fitting case.

After arranging casting the lines and weights with no bait, he placed the rods and reels in their rocket launcher holders and cranked up the engines. He turned on all his running and console lights and moved the throttle to 2,000 rpm and began to cruise southward to the destination marina. He knew the DEA and others anti-drug agencies regularly had spotters on the beach at nighttime.

What he had to be was to be obvious, which meant staying close to shore so he could be seen by any agent examining boats that time of night. It also meant he had to cruise slowly, check his fishing lines on a regular basis and never go too fast.

Racing along the ocean in the middle of the night would only arise suspicion.

Who would question some sport fishermen they saw, trolling along with all the lights turned on in the middle of the night?

This was the riskiest part of the trip was transporting the drugs down to the marina. At any time, a DEA boat could come flying out of nowhere, approach his craft and ask to board.

If he got caught that would be 10-15years in a federal prison.

Tonight, was easy run, done on a mid-week schedule when the number of agents on the beach that could be positioned near the marinas and inlets were minimal. Good intelligence from an inside police source made for an easy run.

As He cautiously made his way into the dimly lit marina from the ocean, he picked up his night visions and saw the van parked sideways to the dock with two men standing by the vans side door.

As his boat slowly approached the dock, he waited to give the prearranged signal.

Five flashes of light from a small LED device. That meant his pickup party knew there were supposed to be five containers.

He responded by turning the running lights on and off – five times.

He watched the man on the dock closely as one of them placed the small nylon bag on the opposite end of the dock and then walk away from it.

As the boat pulled alongside the dock, he threw out a line to one of the men standing on the dock who secured it quickly to a cleat.

The man in the boat was holding a .357 IMIU Desert Eagle, one of the few semi-automatic pistols that fires the .357 magnum cartridge.

The .357 Magnum cartridges have a positive reputation for stopping power which is why it was in his right hand positioned on the right side of his leg. The trigger was already cocked as he waited to hear the pre-arranged rhyme.

"By the light of the silvery moon" was spoken by one of the men next to the van.

The boater nodded in agreement, and while still holding the gun close, he lifted each container out of the boat with his left hand and passed them onto the dock. A nod of the heads in unison and the van closed the doors with its new valuable cargo inside and drove away.

Only after the van was out of sight did the boater relax and walk over to the end of the dock to pick up the bag left by the van's driver.

He decided not to release the hammer on the Desert Eagle until he was out of the marina and back into the ocean.

Going north, he observed the same routine, as he did before on his way south earlier in the night. Fishing rods were all in their holders, running and cabin lights on while cruising north all the while smoking his pipe, sipping on some coffee.

An hour later he had returned to the Atlantic Country Club Members Dock. He hosed down the boat, folded the fishing gear into their Travel Packs, gathered his belongings and left.

Another great night. The Fishing was fantastic. He made $25,000 from his catch.

This was 7 weeks in row netting over $150,000. Much better than his day job.

Chapter 16

It was Wednesday or hump day. Wednesday was always a strange day for me. I didn't know whether to finish up work I had started with clients on Monday and Tuesday, or plan what I was going to do on Thursday and Friday. In any event I had decided to think about it.

Which is really a nice way to say I was unmotivated about work.

I got on my bike and rode about 3 miles through some neighborhoods thinking about Brenda's murder and my conversation with Rodney Filstrom. From our conversation it was only logical – at least in my mind, that he had killed Brenda. Maybe she heard him talking about a drug deal he was involved in? Maybe he was in partnership with Tobias Underwood? What was Tobias doing in the middle of the night at the Members Dock. About the time I had the murder solved, my cellphone rang. It was Lt. Hahn.

"Matt, I got that registered gun report back you asked about."

"Great! I knew one of them owned the .22!" I proudly stated to Hahn.

"Wrong, Mr. Shit for Brains! Neither Tobias Underwood nor Rodney Fillstrom has a registered handgun in their name, or even a family member's name. Do you want to tell me why you think either one of them had anything to do with the murder?" Hahn asked.

Seriously? My theory on who did it was evaporating with each word from Dave.

"Dave, when I talked to both about Brenda, they were almost glad she was dead. Their attitude was so devoid of any emotions. In fact, they acted like she deserved It.", I said.

"Plus, I followed Tobias last week and he had some type of late-night dealings down at the members dock. When he got off the boat, he had a small briefcase."

"Matt, the DEA just told me this morning their informant told them another cocaine shipment came in last night! Plus, the informant said some dumb rich dude's boat from a club was being used in part of the transporting of the drugs."

"Any real reason you suspect members from our club, Matt", I asked.

"Matt, I've got an unsolved murder at your club that looks like it was a hit by a professional.

I got some quasi-reliable intel that mentions a yacht club involved in cocaine transport. And your club is the only one that has a jetty and a small marina built on the ocean. And now you're telling me you've been watching a club member who's doing something strange in the middle of the night on your dock."

"Hahn, it's all circumstantial", I said.

"You're right, so watch out, and keep your eyes and ears open Matt. And the next time you decide to follow someone in the middle of the night, don't tell me about it unless you have something real to report", Hahn said.

"By the way, you and Connie want to go get some dinner and a movie with me and Susan on Saturday night?" Hahn asked.

"yeah, sounds like fun, I'll check with Florida's top vet and get back with you" I said.

After I explained what I had seen with Tobias and his late-night adventures, I quickly realized I had no real evidence of anything except my own self conceived notion of his guilt. All I saw was that Tobias took a small briefcase from the boat that night, which was not a million dollars' worth of cocaine.

Got back on the bike and put the cellphone in my back pants pocket and rode home. The rain clouds were building to the north and I could smell rain in the air. I probably butt dialed a bunch of people on the way back home, but I didn't care.

Murder and drugs at our Club. Really?

I had to find out more. But how?

When I arrived back at the house, Winston already had lunch prepared for me. Like all the meals he prepares for me, healthy is the major theme. Cottage cheese, fresh strawberries, cold breast of chicken, two Oreos and a glass of iced tea were all ready for me by the pool.

Winston is one of those people who can do a multiple activity extremely well and talk at the same time.

As he placed the tray on the table and opened the umbrella he also announced, "Dr. Connie phoned earlier and asked that I tell you to return her call when you arrived", he stated.

Before I could respond, he placed the house phone down on the table, handed me a piece of paper with her number on it and looked at me with that one eyed patch that said, 'call her now'. Satisfied I understood, he did an about face and walked back into the house.

Connie answered her phone and reminded me she had the afternoon off and did I want to go do something fun with her. Yes, I did!

In fifteen seconds of conversation on the phone with her, it was clear that what I had in mind for fun - was not what she had in mind.

"I'll pick you up in 30 minutes. With the rain coming in I thought we'd head over to the mall. There are a few things I wanted to pick up and you can reaffirm my good taste in clothes", she said.

Yeah, just what I had in mind, a mall crawl to several women's stores, where no matter what my fashion opinion was, it would be wrong.

I thought I'd ask how red, or black 6-inch stiletto heels are not in fashion for today's modern woman?

This day was going to be a waste.

Chapter 17

The owner was proud of his new investment. His "Agency" business was good. Cash was plenty. And now he could continue to expand. A new 36-foot sport yacht. Form and function. We're often told we must pick one over another. Not so with this boat.

This is where stylish aesthetics for the jetsetter and power for the explorer combine in perfect harmony.

Cruise your yacht to the places where business can be conducted, and when you arrive, entertain with ease in your transom gourmet center.

First-class amenities in the cabin that stretch from the island-style bed to the gorgeous salon where conversation flows with ease and business can be conducted in private and comfort.

His agency business was run with great professionalism.

Once he decides to hire an escort, she will provide photographs or pose with a special photographer. These pictures are posted on the agency's website or circulated among clients to promote business.

His agencies maintain private websites with photo galleries of their escorts. Clients contact his agency by telephone (recorded) and offer a description of what kind of escorts are sought.

Then he will suggest an escort who might fit that client's need.

His agency collects the client's contact information and contacts the escort.

To protect the identity of the escort and ensure effective communication with the client, his agency arranges the appointment time, location, and the exchange of money. Always in cash, cashier's checks, or the occasional corporate credit cards for the well-known client.

The use of credit cards yields a receipt from a make-believe dentist – for the fitting of a new crown. It's an obvious amount that causes no suspicion.

Sometimes, the escort can contact the client directly to plan for the location and time of an appointment. The escort is also expected to call the agency upon arrival at the location and upon leaving, to ensure the safety of the escort.

Having an Escort's Agency, he had differing fees depending on the season, or whether the client is a regular or semi-regular customer.

His escorts may contract with him to see "clients" for extended meetings involving dinner or social activities on his yacht. For that he charges an additional "user fee".

His agency escorts tend to be split into two categories.

The first is less expensive services, especially if mainly an "in call" appointment. The client is visiting the escort at her accommodation., often only provide sexual services. Also, he provides "outcall" appointments. This is where the escort is visiting the client at either their home or hotel. Both service fees are in the $1200 plus range.

His agency also provides escorts for longer durations when the escort may stay with the client or travel along on a holiday or business trip. His agency is paid a daily fee of $2500 for this booking in advance, and the customer must negotiate any additional fees or arrangements directly with the escort for other services that are not provided in advance by the agency involved.

His escort services charge anywhere from $400 to more than $1500 per hour.

He has a 4-hour, $1500 minimum per, "appointment" fee. The industry standard for dividing the money is 50% to the escort, 40% to the agency, and 10% to the booker (a kind of sales representative). He was the agency owner, and he had a great sales rep in Don.

Don made no less than $3000 a week, he but wanted more.

And Don had a plan.

Chapter 18

Connie had just finished trying on some dressy blouses that would be fun for evening wear. And as practical as she was, she would also wear them under a blazer while she taught a few classes at the university's vet school. They all looked great on her. And why not? She was 5'7", long strawberry blonde, with a slight a flip at her shoulders, a great body, and super curves.

I was lucky to have such a knockout on my arm. With her great sense of fashion and style, I still couldn't understand how she passed on the stilettos!

As we stepped onto the escalator going down, Connie leaned over to me and said,

" Matt, isn't that Tobias Underwood coming out of the store?"

Sure enough, not only was it Underwood but he had an extremely attractive mid-thirties woman on his arm. And she had one of those large "pink" bags that let's everyone in the mall know where you just bought your sexy underwear.

"Connie, that's not his wife or a daughter!" I blurted out.

"I don't know who she is, but I love her taste in shoes," said Connie. "Those shoes are gorgeous and no less than $1800", she continued.

Marilyn Monroe had once said, "Give a girl the right shoes, and she can conquer the world."

It seems Marilyn wasn't alone in her undying admiration for a fabulous pair of designer shoes.

"Matt, those famous red soles, Christian Louboutin shoes are also called, "follow me shoes".

The designer, Christian Louboutin, once said his aim is to "Make a woman look sexy, beautiful, and make her legs look as long as he can.""

"Take it easy sweetie", I suggested. "I agree, they look great, and I love the high heel but you're almost drooling", I said.

Connie responded with, "Matt, besides the shoes, she's got a Tory Burch handbag that's no less than $500. Between her shoes and handbag, you're looking at a $2500."

"I'd like to follow them for a while and see where else they go in the mall", I asked.

"Sure, this is fun and I'm dying to see if he buys her anything else" she said.

Somehow, I felt me, and my Visa Card were in for some trouble!

We followed them from a safe distance halfway down the mall. It seemed as if they were not just shopping but walking as if they were on a mission.

Tobias's cell phone rang, and he pulled it out of his pocket. He laughed into the phone, said something to "Ms. Fashion" that was holding onto his arm and turned around in front of the Coach Store.

And to our surprise, another mid-thirty attractive woman steps out and plants a nice peck on Tobias's cheek as well as Ms. Fashions. It was obvious to Connie and me they all knew each other.

She was the same cookie cutter mold of a woman as the first woman with Tobias.

She was Tall, very fit, and very shapely with natural blonde hair in a ponytail. The black jeans she was wearing, fit her body well with a flowing white blouse that accented her curves.

I must have been staring as Connie poked me in the ribs and stated, "Easy boy, she's another one out of your league, she's a professional."

"You can't afford this one either" she said. "This one's got great taste in shoes as well.

I'd kill her for those Manolo Blahnik.

Spanish designer Manolo Blahnik is one of the few designers that is known specifically and only for shoes."

… "and she's got a large bag from the Coach Store. There's no bag that big from there that's less than $600. You're looking at another $2500-woman, Matt".

Suddenly I felt stupid about women's fashions and glad Connie was with me.

But what was Tobias doing with two great looking women on his arm in the middle of the mall?

"Matt, I don't know if he's their Sugar Daddy, but these women he's with have a great sense of fashion and style. If I didn't know better, I'd bet they're a group of awfully expensive working girls", she said.

Connie and I decided to continue following Tobias, his harem and see what developed. All three of them continued to walk briskly talking, laughing, and approaching the center of the mall.

They all stopped at once, appeared to say goodbye, and the ladies headed to the exit.

Tobias turned away, walked over to the nearby food court area, and greeted his wife!

"Are you kidding me?" Connie said. "this guy just had two very attractive pros on his arms, walking through the mall with no apparent worries and then meets his wife in the same mall for a fast-food lunch?"

Tobias greeted his wife with a nice kiss on the cheeks, sat down and began to eat lunch that Mrs. Underwood had ordered while waiting for him. They were engrossed in some conversation for twenty minutes or so when they finished lunch. Each of them exchanged goodbyes and walked away in separate directions.

Connie and I followed Tobias at a distance and watched him exit the mall, got into his car, and drove away. But to where?

Connie with a perplexed look said, "Matt that was really a strange series of events, don't you think? An old, short balding guy with two babes on his arms, shopping for expensive items, says goodbye and casually meets his wife two minutes later?"

I was baffled at what we had just witnessed. Geez Tobias, was it your cologne?

All I know was that I was glad to see some women wearing a nice stiletto.

Connie and I went back into the mall, finished some shopping she wanted to do and headed back to my place.

The rain had stopped, and the last part of the days sun was beginning to come out. The steam was beginning to come up from the wet streets as the temperature rose. I suggested a swim and some dinner. As we drove over to her place to pick up a change of clothes and her swimsuit, I called Winston and told him we were headed back home for a swim and ...

Already anticipating my next request, he interrupted and suggested Dr. Connie stay for dinner. He would prepare a vegetarian lasagna, a chopped salad, sliced zucchini sautéed in olive oil, toss in some Italian herbs, and top it with a bit of Parmesan cheese. For dessert he would serve cheesecake topped with dash of Chambord, a raspberry and blackberry liquor.

Winston's culinary skills never ceased to amaze me. The dining room table had been set for dinner with a nice bouquet of fresh flowers.

While floating around in the pool, Connie and I explored various options on what we had seen with Tobias during the day. Between the two of us, we had all sorts of theories as to what we saw and what we thought. Everything from the sublime to the ridiculous.

Connie had several early morning animal surgeries scheduled for the next day, so we agreed on an early evening. Connie had picked me up earlier in the day, so she was going to drive back to her place. I was hoping she would spend the night, but the dedicated vet said she needed to do some research before the morning. Sometimes I hate research activities!

Connie tracked down Winston in the kitchen and gave him a nice big hug and peck on his cheek, thanking him for a great dinner. He blushed, regained his composure, and stated she was always welcome, and it was a pleasure to be of service to her.

And in his normal "plan ahead mode" he had prepared and packed extra lasagna and cheesecake for her to take for lunch tomorrow. The man thought of everything, including wrapping up the flowers from the dining room table in a nice bundle for her to take home.

As we walked to her car in my driveway, I asked her about those Christian Louboutin shoes.

"Connie, are those shoes really that special, and are they really worth the money?" I asked.

As Connie got into her car, she looked at me and replied,

"Matt, you'd be amazed at what a woman would give you in return for buying her a pair of those shoes!" Her left eyebrow rose, and a devilish smile came over her face.

In that same instant I knew exactly what I would be buying for her upcoming birthday!

I was glad we went shopping. I'm glad I saw stilettos in action.

Chapter 19

The events of seeing Tobias at the Club dock still were on my mind. What was he doing there at that time of night? What business could he possibly be conducting from midnight to 1:30 am?

I decided to drive down to his office in Fort Lauderdale and stop in and see him at his office at Ocean Yachts, Inc.

It was a classic South Florida weather day. Plenty of sunshine heading my way, so I put the top down on the Austin. The Austin Healey 3000 was the only car I ever lusted for. Mine is a convertible painted a forest green, with a camel leather interior.

Over the years I've realized that all guys at one time or another lusted for a particular car – for a particular reason.

My desire to own this car started in the 6th grade.

All the boys had a huge crush on Ms. Ronca. She was the art teacher at our grade school, St. Marks. In a school that was full of nuns in their habits, Ms. Ronca was a sight for the eyes to a boy in the eighth grade. Of course, it didn't hurt that she was single, very pretty and "middle aged". Remember, to a group of horny eighth grade boys, a woman in her early 30's was middle age!

She also had a set of cannons on her chest that reminded us of the movie, "The Guns of Navarone".

To watch her walk down the hall was better than watching any Saturday morning movie at the theater. Most of the guys had a crush on her - until that one fateful day that reality slapped each of us in the face.

About four weeks into school, at the end of a Friday to be exact, it happened.

Ms. Ronca was walking down the halls in a hurried pace towards the staff parking lot. We usually hung around after school to be polite young men and say goodbye to her.

But at the very instant we all told her to have a great weekend – he showed up!

He showed up in a Forest Green Austin Healey 3000 with camel leather interior and the convertible top down, smoking his pipe, He was there to pick up "our prize", Ms. Ronca.

In our minds it was, "Hey, Ms. Ronca, give us four years and we'd have the car for you as well. Just wait for one of us. Not him"!

As friendly as she was, she announced to us, "bye boys, see you on Monday. My fiancé Scott and I are going to Key West for the weekend. You all have a nice weekend!"

Boys? Fiancé, Austin Healey? Key West for the weekend! Who said she could have a fiancé? What about us. We were all in love.

As they drove off, I knew, the only way to get any woman like her and that was to own a Forest Green, Austin Healey 3000 with camel tan leather interior.

And from that day on, my life's goal was to own one.

My car is not fast, but it always looks like it's going a hundred miles an hour when its parked. It is a head turner. But I've enjoyed the low to the ground ride and the throaty sound coming from the exhaust that only an English Racing Car can make, as you shift through the gears.

When I arrived at the Ocean Yachts office, I was hoping that Tobias would be there. I felt I would have an edge if I showed up and he was not expecting me rather than him waiting and preparing for me.

Their offices were classic yacht brokerage. Soft blue walls, trimmed in walnut. A group of tasteful nautical prints and ocean charts all mounted in cherry frames on the walls. In his office, more of the same with select objects from larger ocean vessels. A large brass porthole which was now a frame holding a picture of him and some boat. A large old ships compass mounted on a brass and copper stand was in the corner. There was also an antique brass and copper fire extinguisher with the top removed that was holding a couple of umbrellas that was next to his desk. Two deep red leather club chairs were in front of his desk with a small mahogany table between them.

"Matt, what a surprise to see you! What brings you to my office? Looking to be become part of the beautiful people and acquire a vessel"? as he shook my hand.

Tobias was one of those people that you wanted to wash your hands off immediately with alcohol as soon as he shook your hands.

"No, Tobias, I'll leave you with the beautiful people." I continued, "I was in the neighborhood running some errands and thought I would stop in and ask you a question that's been on my mind" I started.

"We have a really nice jetty and marina at the club. Do you ever think many of our members use the dock late at night?' I asked.

"The reason I ask, is that with the murder of Brenda, I wonder if adding security patrols to the club and dock would be a good idea if many members did their boating or entertaining late at night on their boats."

Tobias instantly got very agitated, turned away from me and headed over to a small tray that had bottles of scotch, bourbon, and vodka. As he began to pour, he asked," Tucker, want a drink?" Hmm, now it was Tucker, not Matt.

"No, a little early for me Tobias, but go ahead and fix yourself one".

As he poured, I could see his eyes squinting as if he were in deep thought. "Tucker, I don't know of anyone who uses their boat or the dock late at night. In fact, the latest I've ever been at the dock myself has been 930 pm. There's really no reason or desire for anyone to be out there any later. Too dark to see what you need to see", he said.

"Really Tobias? I thought you of all people, a yachtsman and a yacht broker would enjoy late night boating, fishing or some evening selling activity", I said.

"Tucker, anything past dark and I call it quits. No damn reason for anyone to be out on the dock that late after dark. No security needed. That would be a real waste of club funds." With that statement he downed that shot of scotch and then continued. "I guarantee you could wait all night and never see anyone down there. Nice thought, but totally unnecessary. Forget it."

Why would this guy lie about this? Just Last week I saw him on the dock late at night and now, less than a week later he was telling me he's never down there after dark?

I thought I'd probe just a little more and see what his reaction would be. Something was wrong and I wanted to find out what was going on.

"Tobias, I appreciate your insight on the club members boating activities and keeping an eye open for ways to save the club from undo expenses like evening security patrols. But I was just wondering what Brenda was doing down there late at night. Did a club member ask her for some food and drink service, or was a member entertaining on their boat? And does this happen very often that we should consider a part time security guard during the late-night hours to keep an eye on the dock and the club members boats?"

Blurting out and rather loudly, Tobias stated, "Tucker, I told you, no one uses the dock or the facilities late at night. Our members are too old, too busy and we wouldn't need any protection to guard the few boats we have there," he was almost shouting.

Tobias was now looking me straight in my eyes – almost a stare down glaze.

"Take tonight for example; you think there are any members going boating after nine o'clock tonight. Hell no!   Do yourself a favor. Like everyone else, stay home tonight, watch Thursday night football on your television, have a beer and leave the security of our little dock to the pelicans and sea gulls."

He turned to the liquor tray and began to pour another one.

"Tobias, if anyone knows what hours a yachtsman keeps it'd be you. I guess Brenda was" …

He jumped in with," that damn waitress was nothing more than a victim of some illegal person hopped up on drugs, wandering around who tried to rob her to buy more drugs" he stated.

Sensing his strong reaction, I decided to back off and slow it down. "Yeah, you're probably right Tobias; no security guard is needed for late night at our little dock."

Maybe no security guard was needed, but the way he emphasized that I should stay home tonight and watch football tonight, made me think – maybe – just maybe I was going to be hugging a hibiscus bush in the dark at the club dock tonight.

Chapter 20

In a previous life, "helping" our government, I had been given a nice pair of Night Vision Goggles. I still use them on a regular basis when the situation calls for them. Tonight, was a situation.

The GHB-VS 19 is an extremely versatile, military inspired night vision device that can be hand-held and head-mounted using the included head gear or helmet mount, or weapon mounted. Also, it is photo/video adaptable. Tonight, there would be no weapon, no helmet, just me hiding in the bushes near the dock house by our club marina.

I decided I would get to the dock area and be positioned about 930. I was thinking that if Tobias and his company's' late night rendezvous last week was any indication of regular timing, I'd want to be in place early and hope for the best.

The temperature had dropped, and I could see clouds rolling in from the east. Not much of a moon but the light breeze spreads that familiar sea salt ocean aroma in the air.

About 1130 pm and I was beginning to think I should have stayed home and watched the football game. I'd already had 3 cups of coffee was taking a leak against the storage wall when I hear a car door slam.

Put my pecker back in the warmth of my jockey shorts, zipped up my pants and turned on the night vision goggles.

Sure enough, it was Mr. Yachtsman himself – Tobias Underwood walking to the dock, talking into a cell phone. So much for his proclamation this afternoon that he never goes to the dock after dark.

As he walked toward the dock, he was talking into his cell phone. As I was watching him from behind the bushes, it was then I heard the faint sound of an engine in the distance, but not too far away. The sound was growing stronger, which meant it was getting closer. Within 5 minutes I could see the outline of a medium cabin cruiser approaching from the south and was parallel to our jetty. No running lights, no cabin lights.

When Tobias had reached the dock, he pulled out a small flash and waved it the direction of the boat. Immediately running lights came on and a series of console and cabin lights lit up.

The boat made the turn around the jetty and was headed towards the dock where Tobias was standing. A line was thrown out from the back of the boat; Tobias grabbed it and tied the line to a cleat. Then another line was thrown from the front of the boat and he tied that line off as well.

My night visions were turned on and I could see that a tall woman had been piloting the cruiser. And as I watched, it seemed as if no one else was on board.

Tobias stepped onto the back of the boat and the tall woman followed him down into the boat shutting the galley door behind them and turning off the running lights. The faint glow from the cabin lamps showed through the curtains that had been drawn.

Darn.

I waited to see if there would be anyone else joining Tobias and his "friend". After about an hour I decided I would investigate a little closer and take a chance trying to hear anything if I got closer to the boat.

Just as I was about to leave my spot in the bushes, I heard the engine noise of a motorcycle approaching through the driveway coming towards the dock. Whoever was on the bike, killed the lights and engine while he glided into a nearby parking space.

Looking around he seemed to be looking closely at Tobias' car and then started to stare in the direction of the boat that Tobias and his "friend" were in.

But he didn't get off his cycle, but simply nodded, wrote something down on a small notepad, and carefully tucked it in his pocket. He started up the motorcycle and wheeled away.

I decided to stay put. About 15 minutes later, Tobias came out of the boat's parlor and onto the back deck area holding a small briefcase. He climbed out of the boat and onto the dock and began to untie the lines holding the boat in place.

His friend, started up the engines, used the bow thrusters to turn the boat around 180 degrees and headed out of the dock area towards the inlet to the ocean.

Not waiting to watch her to navigate the boat into the ocean, Tobias walked briskly towards his car, threw in the briefcase, and drove off.

Darn, another night rendezvous and I still had no idea who was in the boat, or what was in those briefcases that Tobias received each time he left the boat.

Chapter 21

After a lousy night of sleep, I decided to take a swim in the pool to help me wake up. I came downstairs about 7:45 and Winston was at the kitchen table reading the newspaper.

"Late night Mr. Tucker? he asked. "It was about 2 am when I heard you come in sir. Everything alright"?

"Actually no" I responded. Then I shared with him about the two nights I had watched Tobias and his adamant denial of any late-night activity.

"I've watched him two nights and I still have no idea what's going on." I blurted out.

"Mr. Tucker, might I suggest that the next time you're going to put someone under surveillance in the dark, you elect to bring along a support piece of equipment. Perhaps you'd like to borrow my Walther P-22 pistol with the Yankee Hill Machine suppressor?" he calmly asked.

"Thanks Winston, but if I carry and get caught, I don't want anything coming back to you."

"Sir, you know I'm here for you, when and if you need my assistance. I've been there before and would gladly go there again" he stated.

I knew that he would because he always volunteered to come along. Truth was, I wasn't sure what I was doing except chasing a strange situation and trying to make sense of it.

Thinking about the visitor that came and went last night made me think Winston was right.

So, I went into my bedroom, reached under the bed, and pulled out a small box.

In the box was my "assistant", that the government had just provided me a couple of years ago. It was a new Ruger SR 45 Centerfire Pistol. It's a 45 caliber, with a Black, High Performance, Glass-Filled Nylon, 10 +1 capacity and only 30 ounces.

Lt. Hahn and I had gone to the shooting range just last week during lunch. Each of did well, but Hahn outscored me by 3 points. I'd have to work on my shots to the upper torso.

I'd cleaned and oiled the gun before putting it away like I always do. I checked it for weight and balance again, put it back in the box and slid it under the bed.

Okay, Winston's right -next time, I'll take it with me for comfort.

Chapter 21

Riding my bike over to the club took about 10 minutes. When I got there, I was hungry and decided to stop in the Grill Room. It is less formal and usually filled with good Catholics still eating fish on Fridays. I decided on a bagel, cream cheese, lox, raw onion, and capers. I may not be Jewish, but no one said you had to be to enjoy that!

At a table off in the corner I saw Henry Kane pouring over a group of papers and shaking his head with a perplexed look on his face. Henry was a quiet fellow, late 60's, retired as an actuary from a large New York Investment firm. He was a widower, no children, and a member of the Club for the last 5 years.

He really enjoyed his boat and always offered to help any club member with their new boat.

"Henry, you look like you're back as an actuary fighting the figures", I said.

"Hey Matt, how are you"? He responded.

"Fine, but you look pretty distraught – anything wrong?" I asked.

"Yeah, you know I bought that new Grady White about 4 months ago from Tobias Underwood. Well, today I took it out for a run and noticed the engine hour meter was higher than my logbook or the meter on the dashboard. When I bought the boat, I decided to have a backup meter installed at the engine. I thought that way it would be easier to sell or trade up in the future. Plus, the "technical" part of my personality thought a backup meter was a good idea. Every time I head out, I record the information when I get back, but the engine meter seems 15+ hours higher than my logbook or the dashboard" he said. "Can't figure out how I'm off on the hours".

"On top of that, it seems I'm using a lot more fuel that the specs say I should be using."

"Maybe you went out a couple of times you forgot to record a trip, or maybe the trip was longer that you thought", I said. Of course, I felt stupid suggesting to an actuary that he recorded his information incorrectly. But I had no other answer for him.

"Matt, I always write down in my logbook when I go out, and then when I come back in.

Could the meter on the engine be running in error"? He asked.

"Well Henry, here comes Tobias and a guest, go ask them", I suggested.

"Good idea Matt, I think I will! Have a great lunch. By the way, anytime you want to go out with me for a cruise, let me know. Next week I'm going to make a nice high-speed run down to Fort Lauderdale and open the engines up. I'd enjoy your company" he said.

"Henry sounds like fun, call me and I'll go with you. I've only heard about the performance on that boat so when you give her the full throttle I'd like to be there".

As I walked away, I saw Henry approaching Tobias and his salesman. Somebody better have a good explanation because a senior actuary just doesn't make mistakes. Maybe it's a faulty engine meter, who knows.

I'm sure Tobias would have answer or inspect the meter to see what the problem was.

Chapter 22

When I got back home, I walked into the kitchen to get a glass of water. Winston had most of the kitchen knives on the counter and was sharpening them. Something intimidating about a 6'3" man, with a red beard and an eye patch who is sharpening the kitchen knives with the sound of the blades against the sharpening wheel.

It was at that moment I was glad he worked for me and that he liked me as much as I liked him.

I told him I had lunch at the club and there was no need to fix me anything. And in passing I shared my conversation with Henry Kane and the "missing hours and fuel".

"Sir, an actuary with his experience would not make those types of errors. It sounds to me like someone is using his boat without his knowledge", Winston stated.

Of course! Why didn't I think of that?

"You're right Winston, that's the most logical answer" I said. Winston went on to explain something remarkably similar happened to an associate of theirs when he was working for the Bennett's Company in Africa. One of the local managers had purchased a boat for water skiing. But every two weeks or so, the tank was low on fuel. At first, they thought it was a case of gas theft, but they noticed the real difference when they took it in for some work and the engine meter was higher than the owner's log.

Over a period of 3 months the engine meter reading was continuing to read much higher than the owners logbook. They did some amateur spying and caught him one Saturday evening as he was taking out some people. It wasn't too long before they found out a fellow worker was hot wiring the boat and using it for his own pleasure.

Seems like the guy was doing some low-level smuggling of precious stones on his day off.

Winston was right! That made perfect sense; someone was using Henry's boat. But who was using it and why?

Now I began to think about Brenda's murder on the dock, Tobias, and his evening rendezvous a mysterious man showing up on a motorcycle late at night and Henry's boat being used without his knowledge.

The club's dock had more going on and the pelicans weren't talking.

Chapter 23

Connie and I had a date night scheduled for tonight. We were going out on a double date with Dave Hahn and his girlfriend, Susan. The matter of transportation came up. My Austin Healy was good for two people, so that was out. Dave drove a police officer issued unmarked Crown Victoria, so that was out. Plus, I don't like being locked in the back seat.

Susan is one of the world's worst drivers. She's one of those people that steer where they look. On top of that, she taps the accelerator pedal. No way. Connie has a mid-sized SUV, so it looks like she's elected to drive tonight, which also meant she would be the DD, designated driver – no alcohol for her.

Dave and I let the girls pick tonight's activity, so it was going to be Auggie's Northern Italian. The restaurant is family owned and every one of their employees has spent time in northern Italy learning new dishes and creations.

Despite the long Italian coastline, the cuisine of the north has fewer fish dishes than one would expect. The Mediterranean Sea is generally not as abundant in fish as the Atlantic. In addition, fish was difficult to deliver and never reached the regions in the interior, where fresh water or lake fish are moderately present.

In contrast, the cuisine of Venice is rich in mollusks, crustaceans, sardines, and other fish present in the lagoon. The Liguria region is famous for its cioppino, a fish stew that was transplanted to San Francisco by Genoese fishermen at the beginning of the last century.

 Regardless – I always looked forward to a meal at Auggies'. Especially desert.

Panna Cotta. Sensuously silky and deceptively light, it is also quick and easy to make. I like it left alone – no fancy Mango or Green Tea Panna Cotta for me. Traditionally made in Emilia-Romagna and Piedmont it is a pure, dazzlingly white, slightly wobbly mound, set off by fresh seasonal red or blue berries that add freshness and a little tart accent. Simply delicious!

After dinner we all decided it would be fun catch a late movie. No one had to work tomorrow so staying up late like the "big people" would be a nice change.

After the movie, we decided to head back to my house where everyone had parked their cars. I phoned Winston on the way to tell him we were heading back to the house.

As usual when we arrived, there was a pot of fresh coffee, small pastries and fresh fruit all arranged and waiting for us on the countertop.

"Tucker, do you have any idea how lucky you are to have someone like Winston available to you?" Dave asked.

"Yes, I do! Having Winston here has been a real blessing. Believe me, I know and I'm grateful to the Bennett's for the arrangement", I said.

It was a little after midnight when Dave and Susan decided to say goodnight and go their ways. Connie decided to spend the night at my house, which I was thankful for. We'd been talking about our future as a couple a lot more lately and the thought of marriage was a concern.

I'd already been a lousy husband once, worked too hard, gone too much and I wanted to be sure I had grown up enough not to make the mistakes I made before.

As I looked over at the clock on my nightstand, my mind started to think about the club dock. What was going on there? Who was involved and what were they doing? My mind was full of nefarious thoughts- until Connie came out of the bathroom.

Holy smoke! Connie came walking out of the bathroom towards me, dressed only in one of my white oxford button down shirts, with the top 3 buttons open.

Any thoughts about what was going on at the dock quickly escaped me. I now had more pressing thoughts to deal with!

In a very playful and seductive tone, Connie asked me, "I was wondering if you could have the laundry put a little less starch put in your shirts next time? All of this starch sure makes your shirt scratchy and it's hard to be comfortable in them."

"Well, if you want to take it off, I'll try to shake out some of the starch for you", I replied.

"Well, if you think that will work, I'll let you try that", she said with a smirk on her face. And with that she unbuttoned the last ones, took off the shirt, threw it aside and began walking toward me in bed.

Thank goodness for starch.

Chapter 24

Connie and I slept in until about 830 when we were awakened by the racket of a woodpecker that was attempting to drill a hole into the side of a palm tree next to my window. Not a pleasant sound.

When I was growing up, I would ride my bike over to my grandmother and grandfathers house on Saturdays. He loved birds and had all sorts of feeders, bird houses and bird baths.

I knew that a woodpecker makes the noise for a few reasons. They are trying to attract a mate, foraging for insects to eat or nesting. That would require a hollowed out nesting site, and extensive drilling in one location for a nest. I preferred it not be in the tree next to my window.

While Connie went to take a shower, I went downstairs to see what I could rustle up for breakfast. But as usual Winston was already ahead of me. On the kitchen counter was a pot of coffee and a note from him.

"Sir, went to the grocery for items needed, will return in the afternoon. There is a quiche in the oven, Danish in the box and a selection of fruit in the refrigerator."

I assembled the food and coffee, arranged it on a large serving tray and took it outside to the table by the pool. I started to read the newspaper and pour a cup of coffee when Connie came down and walked over to the table.

"Well, Winston does think of everything doesn't he?" she asked.

Really? Like I was unable to prepare this?

We spent the rest of the morning by the pool, talking about last night's movie and sharing about Connie's latest patients. I never understood how the size of an Irish wolfhound could be in the same breed as a tiny Dachshund.

The subject of the club came up, along with the mysteries at hand that I had been involved in. Connie really wanted me to be careful and to keep my eyes open and be prepared for anything. And she agreed with Winston's assessment, that someone was using Henry's boat without his knowledge.

Just before lunch Connie and I decided to leave my house and walk over to the club. The exercise would feel good, and we could get some sun as well.

We were just outside the driveway entrance to the club when we spotted Tobias and another man standing on the side of the road about 50 yards away. It was obvious they were in some heated argument by the body language, tone, and volume of the conversation.

All the sudden, Tobias pushed the guy forward, walked to his car and slammed the car door shut so hard we thought it might come off the hinges. Without looking, Tobias stormed off at a brisk pace to his car with dirt and gravel flying all over.

The other guy started for Tobias, stopped, put on his helmet, and started his motorcycle. He revved the engine a couple of times and then peeled off down the street. The motorcycle took off with the tires squealing and the cycle sliding left and right as he gained control going down the street.

Tobias acted in a similar fashion, only he headed his car into the driveway of the club at a speed too fast for a country club driveway.

Connie and I watched as he slammed on the brakes in the parking lot, hitting his steering wheel in anger with his hands and then got out and walked into the club.

"Well, that was a little different", said Connie. "Not the same cool, calm and collected guy we saw in the mall last week with the two babes."

"You know, it might be a good time for me to track him down and see if I can learn anything", I said to Connie. "Wanna come along and see what happens?"

"Sure, why not? When my patients get upset all they do is meow, bark, hiss, or chirp! This could be fun and entertaining", she said.

A few minutes later Connie and I had found Tobias at the bar in the Grill Room manhandling a drink with a nasty scowl on his face.

"Hey Tobias, how are you today", I asked.

Without looking up from his drink he tersely replied," Tucker, I don't feel like any damn company right now. I got a lot of things on my mind and being social is not one of them."

As he turned around on his stool, he saw Connie was with me.

"Dr. Stinson, my apologies, I didn't see you there and I should've watched my language. But I've just came from a lousy business meeting and I'm pissed off at his greedy demands", he said.

"Don't worry about me, Mr. Underwood, I was raised with three older brothers and a pipefitter for a father. I've heard all of the words, phrases and finger gestures that were ever created," She was saying with laughter.

I jumped in the conversation with," Well, Tobias, I suspect you've got time to work out compromise or another plan, don't you?

"Wish I did Matt, the sonofabitch wants an answer by this Thursday", Tobias replied.

Thursday! Here we go again; this could be the third time something was going on at the dock. Was it going to be a nighttime adventure again? I decided to cut short this gathering since I had something to plan for.

Thursday night at the club dock was looking like it might be an interesting place.

"Well Tobias, take your time, think about your options and have a good meeting on Thursday night", I said.

"Thanks Matt". Turning to Connie he said, "Dr. Stinson it's always nice to see you. If you ever decide to leave this clown, let me know", said Tobias.

"Mr. Underwood, you're a happily married man, what would your wife think?" Connie said, playing with Tobias and his banter.

"Married, yes, happily no! I'm just an ATM to her.", he said back to her.

"Tobias", I said, "we're leaving before Connie changes her mind. Good luck Thursday night", I said.

He was turning back to the bar and grabbing his drink as he waved us off and said goodbye.

Connie and I left the bar and walked out to the clubs rose garden. It was a nice, secluded area and we talked about the encounter we just had with Tobias.

"Connie, I used the phrase with Tobias, Thursday night three times and he never corrected me. I think something's going down this Thursday. And I'm guessing it may be taking place on the club's dock again."

"Matt, you may be right. Why not have Dave Hahn go along with you as a backup, just in case", she said.

"Connie, Dave can't be there representing the police department unless he has a good reason. Right now, I don't have a good reason for him to tag along. I'll be fine; I just want to see what's going on. I'll be tucked away in some bushes, just watching, nothing more", I said.

Chapter 25

The rest of the weekend was uneventful. And so was the first part of the week.

Until Wednesday.

Henry Kane called me in the morning and told me he had finished up some contract actuarial work he was doing for a client. He wanted to take his boat down to Ft. Lauderdale late morning and wanted to know if I was interested in coming along.

Sure, I was. I had just finished a short bike ride along the ocean and saw that the water was calm. This meant Henry's boat could really fly.

I met Henry at 1030 in the morning and helped him as we prepared to get underway. I watched as Henry went through his checklist. He took out his Logbook and entered the date, time, weather, and guest information. He was as precise as I expected a man like him to be.

Included in that pre-launch, he wrote down the numbers on the analog engine hour meter on the dashboard, as well as the hours that were on the digital meter, he had installed next to the engines.

The weather was perfect, the water was perfect, and this was going to be a great run.

Henry took us out into the ocean and motioned to me he was going to increase the speed. We were sitting in our chairs and bracing our feet as Henry moved the throttle forward. The boat responded immediately, and our speed was rapidly increasing. The boats bow started to rise when Henry moved another lever, planned it off and the bow settled back down as our speed continued to increase.

I glanced over at the cockpit and saw we were running at 40 knots and increasing. Since the ocean was calm and the water was flat, the ride was incredibly smooth over the water.

Henry continued to push the throttle forward and we were approaching 50 knots.

He ran at 50+ knots for a couple of minutes before he backed off the throttle and he settled the boat in at a cruising speed of 40 knots.

Since the water was so calm, we arrived at the marina that he wanted to go to, in about 30 minutes. A nice run!

After we pulled alongside the fueling dock at the marina, Henry turned off the engines.

"Matt, "Would you check the hour meter at the engines and tell me what it says?", Henry asked.

We compared the readings on both meters now as compared to when we left the club dock. The meter readings were 100% accurate and the same as our watches. Both showed a little over 30 minutes or a half hour. Nothing faulty and no discrepancy.

Henry paid for the fuel and we moved his boat over to a temporary slip. The marina had a small restaurant that served mostly great sandwiches, charcoaled grilled hamburgers with great fries and cold beer. I told Henry I wanted to pay for lunch since the boat ride was such a treat.

During lunch he brought up the issue of the different readings on the meters in the past but was surprised and relieved they were accurate on this run. He explained to me that he thought his console gauge was running slow, but on this run it was accurate. Strange!

I chose not to say anything about Winston and Connie's thought that someone was using his boat. No sense in alarming him in just case it was his error.

We finished lunch, got two "roadie" iced teas, and headed back to the boat. Henry went through the same procedure as before. He entered all the data in the logbook, and we took off, including entering the new dual engine meter readings.

The tide was coming in, and the afternoon offshore breeze was beginning to pick up, so the waves were beginning to swell to 2-3 feet. That wave size was nothing for this boat, but Henry kept us at a nice 25-30 knots. It was a fun and physical ride back to our club docks, as the boat lifted off the water on a regular basis.

We got back in a little over an hour as we stopped along the way to give some directions to some boaters heading south from the Carolinas.

After we washed down the boat, Henry took the engine readings again. Same result. Both meters were 100% accurate and in sync with each other – just as before.

We said goodbye to each other, and I thanked Henry for a great boat ride.

Maybe in his advancing age Henry was getting a little confused after all?

It was a little after 230 in the afternoon when I pulled into the driveway at the house. Two items I immediately noticed. One, the fountain in the center of the driveway with the copper dolphin that spits out water had been turned off.

When the spitting dolphin was off, that was Winston's signal for me to be alert.

The second thing I saw was Lt. Dave Hahn's Grey unmarked Crown Vic in my driveway.

Why was Dave here?

Chapter 25

There's an electronic eye at the entrance to my driveway. It's set at 4 foot high so no wandering animal will set it off by accident. Obviously, any car coming on to the property will alert the people inside of the house.

When the driveway alert went off Winston excused himself from a conversation with Hahn to greet me at the front door.

"Sir, Lt. Hahn is here to see you about an urgent manner. He is in the library. I tried to reach you on your cell phone but there was no answer."

I had turned off my phone when Henry and I left the marina after lunch on our way back to the club and had not turned it back on.

"Winston, I turned off the phone while I was with Henry on his boat and forgot to turn it back on, sorry about that", I said.

"Fine, sir," he replied with that disgusted look. "Lt. Hahn is reading this morning's newspaper in the library. Would you like anything?" he asked.

"No thanks Winston, did he say what's up?'

"Something about another drug shipment, sir"

As I walked into the library, I could see Dave was reading the newspaper and had been served an iced tea. Good old Winston, make everyone seem at home.

"Dave, to what do I owe this visit? Anything serious of did you just want to read my paper and drink my tea in a more private setting? Headquarters too busy and noisy?", I asked.

"No smart ass, and its yesterday's newspaper – can you keep up with the latest paper please", he replied.

"Actually, I came over to tell you we got a tip from one of our informants. She tells us there is a good-sized shipment of cocaine coming in sometime before Saturday. But we don't know where or when."

"Dave, that's pretty vague", I said.

"Matt, it does get a little more interesting", he said putting the paper down.

"She tells us it's in this area and she heard it involves multiple transport vehicles. But she doesn't know any more than that. But she did tell us that she heard that some rich people's stuff was going to be used. We just don't know what "stuff" is", Hahn said.

I thought it might be a good time to tell Dave about Tobias and what I had seen. But I also decided to keep the altercation that Connie and I saw with Tobias and some guy out of the conversation for now. Mentioning her would only have Dave following up and talking to her. Plus, I didn't think it was as relevant to his case, as where Tobias' midnight rendezvous at the dock.

"Matt, you're telling me you've seen Underwood meeting up with some boat in the middle of the night at your club dock, and exchanging briefcases and duffle bags – and you just decided to tell me?" Dave was getting pissed off.

"Dave, I was waiting for something more solid than an old man meeting a boat in the middle of the night. Plus, he didn't take anything on board. Nor did he bring anything off the boat except a small briefcase. Nothing that would hold any large amount of drugs or cash like you are talking about", I said.

"Well, I'm calling for a surveillance tail to be put on Underwood right away. I want to know what's going on with that guy. He's either part of something or not. And I'm going to find out one way or another" Hahn stated.

"Dave, before you do that, give me until Friday morning. I want to check something out with Tobias. Let me investigate something off the official police record before you put a tail on him. I'll report back to you no later than Friday morning on what I find out, okay? I asked.

"Bullshit! You know something already and you're holding out on me. That's pushing our friendship, pal, and I don't need any more headaches created by some part time rank amateur" he blurted out.

"Hey, first I agree, what I'm doing is part time. But two, I'm not an amateur and you know it. I'm not full time, but I can handle myself. I'm asking you to trust me for the next thirty-six hours Dave."

"Tucker, I'm going to pretend this conversation never happened – until Friday, at 900 am!"

"Thanks Dave, I appreciate it".

"Don't thank me yet. I'm going back to my office where I can read todays paper."

I walked Dave to the front door and said goodbye. I could tell he was uneasy about our arrangement, but I wanted to see what was going on with Tobias. And for some strange reason, I felt Tobias was going to be at the club dock tomorrow – Thursday night. And I was going to be there as well finding out what was going on with Underwoods and his midnight meetings.

I walked into the kitchen to get a drink of water when Winston approached from the laundry room.

"Sir, do you have any idea why Mr. Underwood is at the club dock so late at night?", he asked.

Winston was never really in sight when Hahn came over, but I knew he heard everything. It was no big deal because I'd come to trust Winston on all my matters. Besides, Winston always had some great insight when I was involved in a case.

Both Bennett's always told me, that Winston was more than a confidant. He had great perception on all sorts of matters. And it would be a good idea as time went on, to involve him in my matters -for his guidance as well. If they trusted him with their lives, so would I.

I had taken that advice and they were correct about Winston.

"Winston, I don't see Tobias Underwood as dangerous. I see a greedy, selfish, self-centered pompous ass. But I just don't see him in a criminal mindset involved with drugs", I said.

"Sir, if I may. Men like Mr. Underwood never seem to have enough. They want more. More money, more power, more prestige, and they want more people to be envious of them. My experience has been they really don't care what they do to get, "the more". They just do it.", he said.

I was thinking about what he said as I was leaning on the counter in the kitchen staring into the sink. I was hoping there was going to be some magical writing in the sink to solve this mystery. No such luck.

"Sir, what are you planning next?', he asked.

"Well, the best thing to do is to go with my gut", I replied.

So, my gut shared with Winston that I was going to go over to the club, just after sunset, and plant myself into the bushes next to the shop building that was close to the dock.

I'd felt something about tomorrow night ever since our encounter with Tobias over the past weekend. I'd get there a little early, just after dark and wait for Tobias and his mystery guest.

This time I was going to figure a way to get real up close and find out what was going on.

Chapter 27

Thursday morning brought some light rain. Checking the local forecast, it showed that the showers would be done by noon. Thank goodness. I was afraid if the rain was going to hang around all day that it might cause a delay in Tobias Underwoods plans. If there were any plans?

Around 2 pm, I'd finished working with some clients in the Caribbean. I was exporting some medical equipment for a friend into the clinics around Jamaica. The government had just passed an initiative and my relationship with the minister of health was resulting in some nice sales and fees being paid to me.

Winston walked into the study, which I had converted to an office. I had kept the mahogany desk and matching leather burgundy leather chairs in front of the desk and simply added my files and laptop computer.

"Sir, your lunch is prepared and is on the dinette table next to the kitchen. I need to go out for a while and get some things we need', he said. "Is there anything you need, sir?"

"No, Winston, I'm okay, thanks for asking. I'll see you later before I head over to the dock."

Connie called me about 5 o'clock and asked how my day went. She'd had a light afternoon. Seemed like all the dogs, cats, hamsters, and snakes were healthy today. She was going to leave her office early and wanted to know if I wanted to get a quick bite for dinner.

"Sorry, babe, remember? This is the night I'm going over to the .club dock and see what – if anything – is going on with Tobias."

"Hey, Matt, be careful. I never like this private eye stuff you're doing. Call me when you get back home. I don't care what time it is; I just want to be sure you're okay" she said.

"I'll be careful. Don't worry I just want to know what's going on."

It was about 930 pm when I finally got situated in the bushes by the north end of the boathouse. From this vantage point I could see into the back of the boat. But just before I settled in the bushes, when it was dark, I had placed a Remote Wireless Surveillance Voice Bug Recorder on the pier closest to where.

I remembered where the center of the boat was last time and where it might tie up.

I owned a "bug" with narrow pulse that will transmit a wireless signal technology, which comes in handy for high-speed, short-distance wireless personal communications. The radius: 500 meters, Pickup: 100 square meters, with 40 hours long standby.

Somehow, I was going to hear what was going on.

Tonight, was going to be my lucky night – I felt it.

About 1030 I heard a car drive up to the dock. Door slammed and the lone man began to walk towards the dock. I had my night visions and could see it was Tobias. He was holding a good-sized flashlight in his hand as he walked towards the dock. He seemed to be taking his time, not in a hurry at all.

When he got to the dock, he sat down his flashlight and pulled out a flask from his shirt pocket. Unscrewing the top, he began to take a belt from the flask while he was looking around the dock and piers. Last time he came, he was in a hurry to meet the boat and get on board. Tonight, it seemed like he was early with no real cares. As he took the first belt of booze from his flask, he spotted something on top of the pier that I had connected the listening device to.

Crap. I left my screwdriver on top of the pier when I installed the bug.

That was an amateur's mistake!

If he continued to inspect the pier and found the device, all bets would probably be off for tonight. But after finding the screwdriver and looking at it, he just put it back on top of the pier as he looked at his watch.

Just when I started to breathe again, I heard the approaching sound of a motor and directed my night visons out to the ocean and back to Tobias. He reached for his flashlight, turned it on, and started flashing the lights off and on for about 15 seconds. The approaching boat responded by turning its running lights off and on a couple of times.

Within the next 5 minutes the approaching boat has entered the jetty and was slowing it engines to an idle, while Tobias was getting ready to help with the docking. A woman appeared from the cabin, tossed Tobias a line and he tied it up on the cleat – right below the pier where my listening device was planted. My estimate where the boat would dock was right on the money. So now my listening device and screwdriver were all in place to record and transmit tonight's business.

Tobias greeted the woman when he got on board with a peck on her cheek and a hug. Nothing real passionate going on here which surprised me.

After all, I was expecting some, wandering hands, suck facing, tongue action.

What a disappointment this was! After they greeted each other, they went inside the main cabin, shut the door, and turned off the boats running lights. In addition, the main salon area lighting was turned down low, but not off.

By shutting the cabin door, it was going to be difficult to pick up and hear anything. I tried to listen and hear what I could pick up, but it was too garbled. After about 45 minutes I decided it was no use. So, I thought I would carefully walk over to the boat and try to listen in by the side of a port hole window.

But just as I was getting ready to come out of the bushes, I hear a motorcycle engine approaching the parking lot from the street. As I turned around to see who was on the bike, I noticed that whoever it was had now shut off the engine and was now coasting into the parking lot-lights off. With the night visions I could only make out a man with a black helmet. He parked next to Tobias's car, investigated the car, and took off his helmet and placed it on the handlebars of the cycle. He was glancing over towards the dock area and beginning to walk in our direction.

Who was this and what did they have to do with Tobias and his woman friend on the boat?

As he was walking cautiously towards the dock and looking in all directions, the main salon lights came on and the cabin door opened. Mr. Cycle saw the lights of the boat and he ducked behind a small garbage dumpster that was on the corner of the driveway next to Underwoods car and his cycle. Then I turned back around to see that Tobias was coming out of the boat. He was talking with the woman as he stepped off the boat and onto the dock.

In his right hand he held a briefcase that he placed on the dock as he began to untie the boat lines. He untied both lines from the cleats, tossed the lines onto the boat, waved goodbye and watched the woman maneuver the yacht.

She knew what she was doing with that boat and she was good. She turned that 38-foot boat around 180 degrees on the spot and then guided the cruiser back out into the ocean and headed south. This time, she had all the running lights turned on as she faded away.

I watched as Tobias picked up the briefcase off the dock and was heading towards his car. He was walking quickly and holding the briefcase close to his chest. When Tobias got within four feet of his car, reaching for his keys, the man on the cycle came out from behind the garbage bin.

In one swift motion, I saw him reach into his jacket, pull out a gun, point it at the back of Tobias's head and then I heard the two Thump- Thumps! A gun with a silencer had just been used on Underwood!

Tobias never knew what happened. The man who came in on the cycle had just put two bullets into the back of Tobias, and he dropped forward like a rag doll. The force of the bullets caused him to rocket forward, and he bounced off his car, face first, and now lay flat on the ground.

He was laying in his own small pool of blood coming from the back of his head into the gravel driveway.

It was obvious the man had used a silencer to keep any noise from the gun being heard.

When a firearm is discharged, there are ways sound is produced. First, part of it can be managed. Muzzle blast generated by discharge is directly proportional to the amount of propellant contained within the cartridge. A small caliber handgun had just been used – quietly and effectively!

As I started to come out of the bushes and raced towards him, I yelled," Hey you stop!"

The man with the cycle heard me and glanced over at me. Then he put on his helmet, grabbed the briefcase, started the motor, and took off down the driveway and onto the street.

He knew I was coming after him and I never had a chance to catch him, get a license plate number or see his face. He was gone down the street in a dark blue cycle.

I raced over to check on Tobias, but feeling no pulse, hearing no breathing, and seeing his eyes were glazed over, it was obvious he was dead. The blood from the back of his head was just spilling into the gravel driveway covering the pebbles around his head and neck.

I dialed 911 and reported the events. Then I asked that Lt. Hahn be notified as well. Within minutes the first officer arrived on the scene and began to ask questions.

Likewise, the EMT's came within minutes, but they saw there was nothing to be done. I watched as they lay a white sheet across Tobias body while waiting for the medical examiner.

While I was never a fan of Underwoods, I certainly didn't wish this type of a death on anyone.

Chapter 28

The officer in charge asked me to stay until the detectives arrived. I agreed and waited quietly in the police cruise until Dave Hahn showed up. All I could think about was what had just happened. Tobias and his late-night meetings, and a mystery man who showed up and killed Tobias. What was in that briefcase to cause Tobias to be assassinated? Money, drugs, jewels? Something had to be so valuable that that it was moved around in the dark of night. And something so valuable that someone would kill for it.

About 20 minutes sitting in the police car, I saw Dave drive up. He got out of the car and walked over to the cop who was writing notes in his daily beat pad. After a few minutes, the cop pointed to me and Dave walked over, opened the car door and I got out.

Leaning against the side of the car Matt started, "Susan and I were watching TV when I got the call. Do you want to tell me what the shit is going on Matt? I agreed to give you 36 hours before I put a tail on Underwood and now you give me a dead guy – who could've been a possible suspect in a drug operation and a murder. Nice going!"

"Dave, let me tell you what I saw."

"Please, Matt, go ahead and shed some light on how a well to do yacht broker ends up the dead – the target of what appears to look like a professional hit."

Just as I was telling Dave what had gone on, I remembered that the surveillance bug was still turned on and attached to the pier on the dock. The crime scene guys were focused on the immediate area of Underwoods car looking for any clues and evidence. Not much to find.

Mostly there was the blood from Tobias head that had spilled onto the pebbles. No real tire tracks could be lifted from the motorcycle and no shoes prints were available because the driveway was thick gravel. What they did find was two spent .22 long rifle shell casings with fingerprints.

"Matt, I gotta have the CSI guys swipe your hands for gunshot residue just to eliminate you as a suspect."

While I didn't mind being swiped and tested, I hated the momentary thought that was in Dave's mind that maybe – just maybe I was the murderer. But within seconds the CSI guys reported to Dave, "No residue on his hands, shirt, shoes or pants!" I was clear-for now.

Dave told me that he had to go over to the Underwoods and tell Mrs. Underwood what happened to Tobias. He asked me if I would go along since I knew her and Tobias. I agreed because I thought Tobias's wife, Bethany Underwood, would be shocked.

Dave got the house number from Tobias cell phone and called ahead and told Bethany there had been an accident that "Mr. Underwood was killed, and he needed to explain to her what happened."

Dave and I agreed that for now, all we would tell Bethany that I was in the area, saw the activity and since I knew the Underwoods, I offered to come along and offer any assistance I could.

When we arrived, the house lights were on and the live-in maid, Bertie, opened the door and was holding a handkerchief, wiping her eyes and nose. It was obvious she had been crying and was upset at the news. She led us into the living room where Bethany was seated, dressed in a full-length black robe, holding a drink. She stood up and greeted us, asking if we wanted a drink, soda, or coffee. We declined and she dismissed Bertie who left the room.

As Dave began to share with her that Mr. Underwood had been shot and had died, she seemed to me like she needed to concentrate on generating some feelings of sorrow and tears. I was surprised there was no anxiety or fits of sorrow coming from her. She did seem more anxious than sorry at her husband's death. What we did get from her was this.

"Lt. Hahn, Matt, thank you for coming over here and telling me what happened to my husband. He was no saint and some of his customers were mad at him because of his dealings with them. I'm not totally surprised. Maybe one of them decided to get even", she said.

Dave asked her the standard questions. Did she know anyone by name that could be that mad at him, was Tobias was having any money problems? Did she specifically know of anyone he had recently had a fight or argument with? Did he use any drugs or spend a lot of time or money gambling and accruing debts?

Finally, and most importantly, did she know any reason he would be at the club that late at night?

We intentionally left out the part about him meeting the boat, dock, and the woman he met along with the briefcase that had been stolen. For now!

Bethany Underwood answered, "No" to all of Dave's questions and said Tobias often went out on Thursday evenings to meet clients.

Really, Thursday nights?

What was he doing on Thursday nights? Before I could ask about why he was out so late she asked something very strange. At least it was strange to me.

"Lt. Hahn, was anything stolen from my husband's car?"

A woman has just been told that her husband is dead, and she wants to know if anything is missing from his car. Not him, but his car?

Dave picked up on her strange question as well. "Like what Mrs. Underwood?"

"Did they take his wallet, or his watch or anything else that would suggest a robbery, like his cellphone or briefcase" she asked.

As Dave was looking at his notes from the officer on the scene, as well as the CSI tech's report of personal effects, when I decided to share some facts and probe Mrs. No Tears.

"Bethany, no one took his watch, ring, cellphone or wallet, the police found all of them, still with Tobias. But I don't remember a briefcase – do you Lt. Hahn"? I asked. "Since nothing of value seems to have been taken, it leads the police to rule out robbery and to explore that this crime against Tobias was something much more serious – perhaps he was murdered", I said to her.

Lt. Hahn asked, "Was there a briefcase Mrs. Underwood? We didn't see one. Do you know for sure that Mr. Underwood had a briefcase when he left the house tonight?"

Bethany seemed flustered and replied, "sometimes he has keeps in his trunk, was there one in the trunk"? She asked.

"Do you know what might have been in the briefcase Mrs. Underwood?" Dave asked.

"When can I have my husband's car back" she asked.

What? When can she have her husband's car back? What about poor Tobias lying on a cold stainless-steel tray in the refrigerator over at the morgue?

Dave's experience had taught him that this type of conversation, especially from a new widow needed more follow up and investigation – but not right now.

"Mrs. Underwood, the crime lab has towed the car down to the police station for a close examination for fingerprints or clues. I'll ask about a briefcase that maybe is in the trunk.

I suspect you can have the car back in a few days along with Mr. Underwoods personal effects" he said.

We said our goodbyes and shared with Bethany our sympathy on her loss. We left the living room, with Bethany still sitting on the couch holding her glass of scotch, as we headed towards the front door.

Bertie the maid stopped us.

"Mr. Underwood always went out late on Thursday's and came back even later. My room is over the garage and I always heard him when he came back home and opened the garage door. I never knew what he was doing out so late – but Mrs. Underwood was always waiting up for him", she said.

"So, she knew he was out late and waited up for him? Was there any fighting when he came back home?" Dave asked.

"No, in fact they'd usually go into the den and have a drink and talk", she said." I know, because I'd hear them talking real quiet like, and in the morning, I'd have two glasses that had some booze left in them to clean up".

"Bertie, on Thursday nights did you ever see Mr. Underwood leave with a briefcase?" Hahn asked.

"No, never, besides, he got five or six of them black briefcase in his office. Don't know why he has so many of the same ones. Don't even look like they've been used," she replied.

Dave looked at me briefly and said thank you to Bertie. He led the way out to his car with me in tow behind him.

We were both silent as we walked to his cruiser. After we got in the car, Dave was about to turn the key on when he paused and looked over at me.

"Matt, she's worried about a briefcase, and the maid tells us there's 5-6 of them in the study. Seems like maybe she was expecting something to be in the briefcases and they're being used or rotated on a regular basis" Dave said.

"I agreed, something was being received or transported in those cases that was of real value. And someone knew what was in that briefcase, which is why they murdered Tobias", I said.

Dave phoned into the police garage and asked the CSI on duty if she would go investigate the trunk of Underwoods car right now and see if there was a briefcase in it and to call him back.

There was nothing more to be done tonight, so Dave drove me home. As we pulled into the driveway the front lights came on, and Winston met us at the door. I asked Dave if he wanted to come in and talk about the case and have a cup of coffee and he agreed.

We walked into the house and sat down in my den. Sitting in the den is always a more relaxing environment to discuss business. My den was walnut paneled from floor to ceiling and furnished with two pairs of large club chairs in dark burgundy leather. The chairs were extremely comfortable and are in a two-by-two arrangement, facing each other with a small mahogany table in between the chairs. Off to the side of the chairs is my desk.

Winston came in and suggested that since the workday was ending for both of us – it was 130 in the morning - that we might like some Bushmills Irish Whiskey in our decaf coffee. We both agreed and shortly thereafter, Winston returned with our poor man's Irish coffees in some white stoneware mugs. Of course, he also brought in cheese, crackers, nuts, and hummus on the serving tray.

Dave and I were talking about tonight's murder when his cell phone rang. He answered the call, listened, exhaled, said thank you to the person on the other end of the call and hung up.

"Matt, no briefcase, only some generic boat papers on vehicles" he said.

We didn't figure there would be a briefcase in the trunk, but we wanted to make sure.

Now what?

Chapter 29

 Since Dave and I had worked into the late night and early morning, I decided to sleep in the next day. It was around 845 in the morning when I walked downstairs into the kitchen and noticed it was raining. On the center of the granite island was a note from Winston telling me he had gone to the store and would return around noon.

Of course, his instructions were laid out for me.

In the refrigerator he had prepared a series of small bowls. There was a small bowl of plain yogurt with three other bowls containing granola, raspberries, and sliced banana. The coffee was in a thermos on the counter, with the mug sitting next to it along with today's newspaper. I was halfway through reading the paper when I heard Winston's car pull in and the garage door begin to open.

"Good morning Winston!" I spoke. "Thank you for preparing some late-night snacks for us-we didn't realize we were that hungry until after we started to eat. Thanks again!"

"No problem sir! While I was at the market, I had a few thoughts on Mr. Underwoods murder and some of the details you and Lt. Hahn shared."

"Yeah – did you come up with any great revelations?" I asked.

"Yes sir, as a matter of fact something has bothered me" he started. "It would appear there are some relevant details about the many briefcases Mr. Underwood has in his den. His maid said they don't look worn, but rather almost brand new and not worn. That would indicate they may be used in one-way transactions. And with Mrs. Underwood questioning the whereabouts of a briefcase, it might indicate, that he was bringing home something on a regular basis not taking it out" he said.

I told Winston that on the two nights I had been watching Tobias, he got off the boat with a briefcase. So, it appeared only a small group of people knew about the briefcase exchange, Tobias, the lady on the boat who gave him the briefcase, his wife, Bethany Underwood, and the mystery man on the motorcycle who murdered Tobias. With five or six briefcases in his den, it might indicate the activity has been going on for five to six weeks.

It seemed the two key elements of this mystery are the lady on the boat and the motorcycle killer. But I had no idea how to locate or identify either one of them or I assumed Bethany Underwood was not going to be of any real help.

Chapter 30

The rest of the day was spent with me finalizing shipping plans for some medical equipment and a desalination water system that was going to Jamaica. Both items had been purchased by their ministry of health from me and immediate delivery was requested.

After completing the customs paperwork and emailing it to the export freight broker I decided to take a quick bike ride. As I walked into the garage, I realized – no bike! In all the haste of last night, I forgot I left my bike at the club. And the planted listening device was still attached to the pier. Oh great, another "rank amateur" move by me.

The rain had stopped, so I jumped into my car and drove over to the club dock.

Of course, the stupid screwdriver was still in place from last night, so I quickly removed the listening device from the pier and drove back home with the bike in my truck.

Connie and I had a date night set for tonight. We were going to get a casual dinner at a small seafood restaurant that was down on the water in Ft. Lauderdale. Later, our routine would be to walk over to Heavenly Delights, a gourmet cupcake place and then see a movie. The cupcakes were okay, but the icing, piled high, was to die for. We had a great seafood dinner. I had the Everglades Boil. Freshly sliced red snapper, shrimp, sausage with fresh green beans with bacon and onion infused with the beans. Bacon should be on everything!

As we walked over to the cupcake place, we noticed a somewhat large gathering of sport motorcycles. From the decals on the side of the bikes, it Look like they were all Ducati's owners. By the way, the Ducati is the perfect blend of tradition and modernity and marks a return of the pure essence of motorcycling: two wheels, a wide handlebar, a simple engine, and a huge amount of fun. Seems like they had been gathering for cupcakes and coffee, having a good time after they had ridden.

As they began to start their engines, I knew that was the iconic sound I had heard last night. Very distinctive. As I looked around, I told Connie, this was the exact outline bike type of last night. But every bike was red, green, or blue. And everyone had helmets.

Now I knew this was the bike type of the rider that killed Tobias. Feeling proud of my memory powers, Connie jumped in.

"Matt, I think this is the same type of motorcycle – same silhouette as we saw last week. The day we saw Tobias and that man arguing in front of the club".

Connie was right!

Approaching one of the riders I asked if they rode as a group often and he replied they have a standing ride set for every Friday. "Whoever shows up, we assemble and ride" he answered. "And because half our group are serious woman riders, we stop by here for cupcakes, coffee or bottled water, but no alcohol, before we all head home" he said.

I made a mental note to call Dave on Monday and tell him about the motorcycle Connie and I had identified.

I knew that this was the make of our murders motorcycle.

This was a classy group of owners and riders - and a member of this group may be the killer.

Chapter 31 Saturday

Connie spent Friday night at my place as she wasn't on call at her office this Saturday. We slept in a little past 830 in the morning when the sound of that darn woodpecker woke us again, outside my window. I swear I'm going to shoot that bird so I can sleep in on Saturday as well as stop the damage he's doing to the stucco.

Connie showered while I went downstairs. Winston was reading the newspaper at the kitchen island and remarked about the papers account about the murder of Mr. Underwood.

"Winston, I'm pretty sure I know the cycle that the killer was on" I said. I related to him the story of last night and running into the group of motorcycle owners at the cupcake shop.

"Sir, as a matter of record, that brand of bike owners tends to be a serious rider. They are extremely capable and careful how they ride. They handle that motorcycle very well and tend to ride in groups for enjoyment and safety. They also tend to be cautious and wear full padded leather jackets and riding boots in case of an accident. It's not a common bike to own unless you are a serious and regular rider."

Where did Winston know this from?

Connie and I had noticed almost everyone had the same motorcycle jacket on, just in different colors. Darn, how did Winston know all of this?

"Breakfast for you and Dr. Stinson will be ready in a few moments out by the pool sir, I'll bring your coffee while you wait poolside?" he stated.

With his statement, I knew I was being dismissed from "his" kitchen. Gosh I love this guy!

Connie came down a few minutes later. She was wearing a nice fitting pair of blue jeans with a nice blue sleeveless polka dot blouse. She kept a few things at my place so she could have a change of clothes when needed. While Connie and I were eating breakfast, we were talking about what to do for an activity today. I told her about the conversation earlier with Winston and asked if she would mind if we went to the motorcycle dealer. She knew I was a little fixated on the case and going to the dealer anyway – so she might as well agree and save the discussion.

Winston located the dealers address for me. As we drove down it seemed like every motorcycle, we heard had a slight difference to their sound. Could really identify the sound as the biker that had killed Tobias or was its wishful thinking.

We arrived at the dealer and pulled into a parking space up front. A group of people were looking at the cycles outside the front door on display and immediately diverted their attention to me and Connie. Were we such a handsome couple or was it the car?

It was probably Connie's good looks and the car – hopefully in that order.

We began to look around. Every bike tended to look alike. Walking into the showroom we noticed the large display of padded leather jackets, pants, and gloves. They were just like the ones we saw last night.

A lady salesperson came up to us and started off with, "HI, I'm Jan. Nice Healey you have. A Mark III Series! Very classy. Now how about a motorcycle as serious as your Healey? She asked.

"Well, you know your cars, but we're new to the motorcycle activity" I said.

Connie jumped in and asked," the bikes look pretty serious for new riders, can two people ride on one together?" she asked.

"Yes, but our owners are pretty serious and dedicated riders prefer to ride single, husbands and wives have their own bikes" she said. "Plus, almost all of our customer ride with full leather pants and jackets in the case of an accident. Not blue jeans and blouses like yours. While you look cute, in an accident, the full leathers offer a much better coefficient of reduced drag."

Coefficient of reduced drag? I want to hear motorcycle engines and find identify a killer, not outfit we with leather or solve physics problems!

Wait a minute. Maybe we can play dress up. I'll be the big bad biker and Connie can be my biker chick. On second thought, forget it; she'll never go for it.

Without missing a beat or objecting to the assumption, Connie was quick on the draw with a response. "Jan, I'm Connie and this is Matt. We're interested in two bikes, but we really don't want a bike that starts up with the loud resonance of a bike big."

Jan was just as sharp and replied. "Connie, I know what you mean, follow me outside and let me start one up for you. You can listen to it and see for yourself".

Jan led us out to a bright red bike, pulled the key out of her pocket and turned it on. As the engine turned over and she increased the revolutions, I knew this was the sound I heard at the club the night Tobias was killed. This was the engine I heard.

Just then, another owner was leaving the parking lot and I listened to him as he took off. It was the same distinctive acceleration sound I heard. This was the make. No doubt about it. Connie nodded to me, and I knew this was the same bike she heard that day at the club.

As if on cue, Connie looked at her watch and told Jan that we had another appointment, took her business card, and told her we would come back another time and possibly get a little more serious.

When we left, I suggested we stop by two other popular motorcycle dealers and listen to the engines. We did. And the sound wasn't close to what I heard that night.

Now we had identified the bike – but how would I find the owner and the killer?

Chapter 32 Monday

On Monday morning I came downstairs and was going to take a nice brisk walk before breakfast. As I came into the kitchen Winston was in his usual pose – standing tall and straight – reading the morning paper. I used to ask him if he wouldn't be more comfortable leaning across the counter instead of standing so erect holding the paper out in front of himself.

His answer was always the same. "Sir, a gentleman does not lean or slouch" he replied.

Sorry, I lean and slouch.

"Sir, Mr. Underwoods memorial service is going to be held tomorrow at Schillings Funeral Home at 7:30 pm. Shall I send some flowers on your behalf?" he asked.

"No, I wouldn't want to do that after I saw a lack of emotions from Mrs. Underwood. Something is wrong with this situation", I said.

Despite the fact I was not a real close friend of Tobias and I was not going to send flowers – I was going to attend the memorial service just to look around and see what I might learn.

What I was planning to do today was to drive down to Tobias's office and talk to his secretary and see if I could learn anything new. But thinking about it I decided it might be a good idea to ask Dave to come along in an official police capacity should I need his "badge".

Dave picked me up at my house after lunch around one o clock. I offered to drive, but he told me if he was going on an official capacity – he better drive his car than sport around town in my Healey.

For a Monday, the parking lot at the Marina and offices seemed to be full and parking spot was a little hard to find. Finally, after driving around the lot a couple of times Dave grabbed a spot about two rows back from the office as an elderly couple pulled out.

Walking into the office we decided Dave would ask his questions and I would fill in where I thought it might be helpful. But we didn't want to scare the secretary.

When we went inside Tobias's reception area, we heard some loud voices coming from Tobias office, and people were arguing about something. It was obvious the secretary was a little embarrassed and quickly went into the office area and announced our arrival.

The volume ceased immediately.

She came out and escorted us into Tobias office. Behind his desk, there was Bethany Underwood sitting and obviously going over a series of papers on his desk.

The guy in the office with her I recognized. But I couldn't remember where I had seen him before. He seemed irritated and put out about our arrival, which could be seen on his stupid facial grimace.

"Mrs. Underwood, let me extend my sympathy at your loss. Please know we're doing all we can to solve this crime for you" Dave stated.

Before anyone else could respond, Bethany Underwood replied in a sharp tone. "Lt. Hahn, while I appreciate, you're trying to do all you can to solve my husband's murder, Tobias was an ass and a self-centered pompous fool. Right now, his sales engineer, Don and I are trying to keep the revenue and clients intact. Do you have any leads on his murder or his briefcase?" she asked.

The briefcase again. What was in the briefcase I wondered.

"Bethany, you've been concerned about the briefcase and I was wondering if you could tell Lt. Hahn and myself what was in it?" I asked.

"Just papers – some important papers on yacht titles and some banking statements" she stated.

Just them, Don Boy, chirped in. Don was about 45 years old, tall, slender with a gold necklace, three rings on his fingers and a gold bracelet on each wrist. I suspected he bought his jewelry at one of those stand-alone discount jewelry kiosks at the mall – and not Tiffany's.

Don radiated the epitome of slime.

"Guys, whoever shot Tobias is long gone. I'd concentrate on the theft of the briefcase. Are you sure no one at the police station may have taken it?" he asked.

Dave had a look on his face, his increasing red face, that reminded me of a soda can that had been shaken and then the top flipped off. It was going to be a mess. But as a true professional, Dave simply replied, "Don, no one at the station took that briefcase. The entire lab and garage are under 24-hour surveillance by cameras." Then he added, "By the way, can you tell me where you were that night between 930-1100"?

Way to come back Dave, I thought!

The reply was a surprise and not by Don.

Bethany replied very quickly – and in my opinion, a little too quickly," Don was with me earlier in the night at our house because we were going over the financing of a recent sale. I was handling the finances from my trust account for the buyer since the bank was taking too long to approve a loan."

"Great, Don, can anyone else corroborate your alibi?" Dave asked.

"Hey since when isn't Bethany's word good enough for the cops?" Don nervously asked.

Bethany blurted out," Don, don't be stupid, the Lt. has to ask these questions. Yes Lt. Hahn, Bertie our housekeeper can tell you that Don was at the house that night doing business with Tobias and myself."

At that moment I decided to change the subject just a bit and asked," Don, what is it you do here at the Ocean Yachts?"

Don seemed to relax, leaned back in the chair and proudly announced, "I do a lot around here. I help sell the yachts, take certain clients out for demonstration rides, instruct them on how to operate the boat and I fix the electronics and gauges on the control panel of the boats if there's a problem. Why I can even reset an hour meter and reduce the hours on an engine. That's not legal, but some other brokers have asked me to do it for them. But I always say no".

Yeah, right, he always says no. I'd bet Mr. Slime alters those hour meters for brokers and people selling yachts – even Tobias.

Dave addressed his next question to both Bethany and Don with, "Tell me, any unhappy clients of Mr. Underwoods that may have been mad enough to come after him?"

Bethany jumped in and replied, "Lt. Hahn, every one of our clients have been more than pleased with their purchase, as well as their after-sale service from Don. Whether it's for business or pleasure."

"Yeah, all of our customers are happy, and some of them even use their boats to earn good cash money", Don chirped in.

What I noticed was how fast Bethany turned her head and looked at Don as he finished his remarks. He just said something that caused her to be very alarmed!

"Lt. Hahn, Matt, if there's no other questions, we'd like to get back to work", she said.

After watching her reaction to Dons remark I decided it was time to bring up the incident in the mall where Connie and I had seen Tobias with two great looking women.

"Bethany, this last question is asked as delicately as possible, as far as you know, was Tobias seeing any other women?" I asked.

Don chuckled, Bethany gave him a sharp look, turned back, and responded with," Tobias always looked at other women, but it was always just a look and business first".

What did that mean?

Chapter 33

Dave asked a few more routine questions, handed Bethany his card and asked her or Don to call with anything they thought of that may help.

We left the yacht offices and were sitting in the car discussing the conversation, when we saw Don come out of the building. He had a black motorcycle helmet in his hand and was wearing a black and red leather riding jacket.

He started his motorcycle and right then I knew!

That was the same sound I heard the night Tobias was shot.

And this was the same sound I heard with Connie at the motorcycle dealer.

Could Don be the killer? But why? What could be his motive to kill his boss? There was nothing to indicate a love triangle between Don, Bethany, and Tobias. Yet all the sudden, seeing Don on that motorcycle had me and Dave focusing on him.

As Dave and I drove away I was thinking about Don. Probably for no other reason that he drove the same type of motorcycle I saw and heard the night Tobias was shot.

"How many engines do you think Don's rigged", Dave asked me as we were driving along the ocean road.

"Probably more than we want to think about" I replied.

Then it hit me.

In a cruise two weeks ago with Henry Kane, he had a curious situation. His engine meters were not calibrating.

"Dave, turn around now and go back to Underwoods office. I just remembered something that I need to ask Bethany that may help" I said.

"Matt, what is it" he asked.

"Don told us that he was a whiz at electronics and engine meters. One of our members, Henry Kane has had a strange thing happen with his boat he purchased recently.

The dashboard engine meter is not in sync with a meter he installed on the engine."

"Are you suggesting Don is somehow involved? He asked.

"I'm not sure but there's one way to get closer to Henry's engine discrepancy, and maybe get us closer to this series of crimes" I said.

We pulled into the parking lot and noticed Bethany was briskly walking over to her car.

"Dave, pull in behind her and follow my lead" I said.

Dave pulled the police cruiser right behind Bethany's car. She saw us in her rear-view mirror as we both got out of the car and approached her.

"Bethany, I forgot to ask a non-related question. You know Henry Kane from the club, right? Did Henry buy his boat from Tobias?" I asked.

"Yes, as a matter of fact, Tobias sold him a boat about six months ago and Don delivered it to him and instructed Henry on its operation, why do you ask?"

"Oh no reason, two weeks ago Henry told me how pleased he was with the purchase of his boat and suggested I look into getting one like his. I forgot to ask who he bought it from" I said.

"Well, if that's all you need, I really need to get going" she said.

"Thanks Bethany, maybe I'll come and talk about a boat with you" I said.

"Talk with Don, he's smart on all aspects of the boats and their operations," she said.

We got into the car and drove out of the parking lot and back onto the beach road.

"What was that all about?' Dave asked.

I told Dave that Henry was concerned about the engine meters not in sync. A senior actuary doesn't make those types of mistakes. I told him that over the last couple of months; maybe Henry's boat was getting used without his knowledge. He was seeing more fuel used and the engine meters were not in sync. And although the last trip he and I took together, the meters were in sync.

I had a theory.

Maybe – just maybe Don was using Henry's boat. But why? And for what? But it did make sense. Don delivered the boat to Henry and knew its working parameters and could alter the electronics.

But for what reason?

Dave and I stopped by the Rusty Pelican Grill on the way back. It was too early for a beer, but we wanted to compare some feelings about the meeting with Bethany and Don.

One thing struck me odd.

"Dave, did you see the reaction Bethany had when Don mentioned clients using their boats to generate cash" I asked.

"Yeah, I did, what the heck was that remark all about" he replied.

" I don't know, but something spooked her with that remark of his" I said.

Dave dropped me off at my house and we agreed that as friends and couples we'd all try and get together this coming weekend. He told me to check with Connie and he'd check with Susan. If the weather was good, we might be able to get in a beach day, some lazy time by the pool, or a nice dinner out on the water somewhere in Fort Lauderdale.

When I walked into the house, I smelled the distinctive odors of two products. The first was the smell of furniture polish and the second was spray starch. Sure enough, in the kitchen was Winston ironing some of his shirts and some of mine.

"Winston, I told you, send the shirts to the cleaners and save yourself the time and effort" I said.

"Sir, I prefer to press my own shirts and doing yours is part of my duties" he said. "Besides, I prefer the way I starch your shirts."

No sense in arguing with Winston, as I've been telling him this every time, I see him iron my shirts.

Remembering last weekend with Connie and her problems with my shirt and the starch – I silently agreed with him.

Keep putting lots of starch on my shirts Winston!

I went over to the refrigerator and poured a glass of iced tea and sat down at the island countertop next to him.

I relayed our interview with him as well as the strange remark Don made that caused such a reaction from Bethany Underwood.

"Sir, do you remember the conversation we had last week about the employee who was using Mr. Bennett's boat in Africa?

Remember, how I told you the employee was smuggling gems and delivering small amounts of drugs at night? Maybe this Don person is doing the same. Maybe he's using someone's boat that Mr. Underwood sold them, and then he alters the electronics."

Winston was on to something. But exactly what it is was still baffling me? Is Don using Henry Kane's boat for something? Or is he using several boats they sold. Is he using them for drug running operations?

But when. And is there some type of schedule?

Chapter 34 Wednesday Night 1145 pm

The thirty-seven-foot yacht was coming into the marina. The boat was painted in a regal blue on the main hull, while the topside was trimmed in a pearl white. It was accented with beautiful teak port holes, windows, and the main cabin door.

Tonight's weather had been perfect for the five-hour ocean cruise. The moon was out, the stars were shining, and the ocean water was calm once again.

As the yacht got closer to its dock space, two middle aged men came out of the cabin area and began to position themselves on the bow and stern of the boat to help with its docking procedures. They each had a rope line in their hands to tie off the boat as it approached its final docking location.

It was obvious to anyone watching nearby; the captain had full control and made the docking maneuvers look extremely simply. The boat barely kissed the buoys as the engines shut down.

The men jumped to the dock and fastened the ropes to the cleats.

Three women emerged from the cabin area along with two more men.

"The captain" that handled the craft so well was a woman in her late 30's, with long blonde hair in a ponytail. They all seemed to be rather quick and cordial with their goodbyes, by gently kissing each man on the cheek and sending them on their way.

While the four men walked down the dock to their cars, the women stayed behind and spent some time securing the yacht.

While stepping off the yacht and onto the dock, the 'captain' announced, "Ladies, well done! That was a $20,000 trip."

As each woman left the boat, they had a large leather bag strapped over their shoulder. Walking into the adjoining parking lot for yacht owners only, each one got into her own car. Two Mercedes, a Jag, and a BMW 6 Series, all left the parking lot together and all of them headed in different directions.

Chapter 35. Thursday

Connie usually takes a long lunch break on Thursdays as she performs a lot of animal surgeries during the day. A longer lunch allows her to regain some composure for the rest of the afternoon.

I decided to try my luck and pick up a couple of nice club sandwiches, chips and bottled water and see if I could interest her in a nice lunch break. She was just finishing some minor surgery on a French Bulldog when I arrived. She saw me at the reception counter and said lunch would be a nice treat. I walked down the hall towards her office and waited for her while she changed clothes.

"Connie, with Tobias dead I didn't really think there is any need to think about Thursday nights at the dock. But for the last several weeks I've witnessed some type of activity and a murder. So, I feel compelled to go and hide in the hibiscus bushes once again and see if anything continues."

"Matt, you may be right, but why not take Dave along with you? I'd feel you're a little safer with Dave alongside you" she asked.

"Well, it does get a little boring out there and some company might not be a bad idea if the night proves to be fruitless" I replied.

Connie shared with me her morning's activity and how happy she is when she can help a hurting pet with a successful surgery. She also shared with me how bad she feels when there is nothing else that can be done to save a person's closest animal friend.

After lunch, we confirmed a nice dinner date for tomorrow night, and I reassured her I would call Dave this afternoon and tell him about tonight and see if he wanted to tag along.

Chapter 36

As I was about to call Dave, my cell phone rang.

"Mr. Tucker? This is Bertie over at the Underwoods, can you come over and talk to me right now?" she asked.

"Sure Bertie, is everything alright?" I asked.

"Mrs. Underwood said she left for the Yacht office and I wanted to tell you something" she said." Can you come right over now before she gets back"?

"I'll be right over Bertie."

What could this be about and why did Bertie want to talk to me - now, I wondered driving over to Underwoods house.

No sooner had I pulled into the driveway when Bertie came out of the front door. As she approached my car, I could see she had small bruise on her face by her right eye.

"What happened to your face Bertie?' I asked.

"You know Mr. Tobias was murdered" she said. "There are some funny things going on here with Mrs. Underwood. Things not right" she said.

"Like what?" asked.

"Well for one, this morning I asked her why she and Mr. Underwood had all of them briefcases in the den and what were they used for? Maybe there might be something in there to help the police find out who killed Mr. Underwood" she said.

"And what did she say" I asked.

"She slapped me hard and told me it was none of my business – to stay out of the den and not to bring it up again, or I'd be fired" she said.

"What do you think might be or was in those cases?' I asked.

"I don't want to get into no trouble, but I think they had a lot of money in them" she said.

"Why do you think that, Bertie?"

"Well, every Thursday night late, Mr. and Mrs. Underwood went into the den, after he got home. Then they closed the door to the den, talked out loud and seemed to be in a good mood."

Bertie continued, "In the morning Mr. Underwood would always tell me he had to go right to the bank to deposit money", she said.

"Bertie, this is a real important question I have to ask you. Did you ever see Mr. Underwood leave the house on a Thursday night - or any night with a briefcase or satchel?" I asked her.

"No Mr. Matt, on Thursdays I always said goodnight to him as he left, and he didn't have no briefcase or bag with him. He only had a case when he came back late at night. I'd see him carry one into the house when he got back".

Great! No exchange seems to be going on, but for some reason, maybe Underwood was getting cash on Thursday nights. But from who? And for what?

And there was still the fact I'd seen the man who killed Tobias and took the briefcase that night.

If it was money in that briefcase the night Tobias was killed, I understood why Bethany Underwood was so concerned about the missing briefcase that night.

.

Chapter 37 Thursday Night

After my meeting with Bertie, I called Dave from my cellphone and told him what she had told me – and how violently Bethany reacted towards Bertie. Bertie was truly scared something was going on in that house and she didn't want to be any part of it.

Dave agreed to come and stake out the dock but that tonight might be a waste of time. But it might be worth it as criminals have a pattern and they hate to break them.

We agreed to meet at 9:30 pm, by the boathouse next to the dock. It was one of those nights with no moon and real dark.

We'd park our cars down the street and walk into the dock area from the north side of the grounds. There was a small entrance along the fence area, and we could walk along the outskirts of the club and not be seen.

Dave got there the about the same time I did, so we split up and entered the dock area one at a time. I went first to make sure no one else was there. If there was, I was a member and could explain my presence easier than a police detective.

No one was around so Dave approached the boathouse after he saw me get situated.

As he was walking past me in the bushed, I grabbed his arm from inside the bushes and pulled him into the area. Unfortunately, it startled him.

"Crap Matt, you want to get shot? Next time just whisper, here I am", he said.

"Sorry, I just didn't want anyone to see us. I'm used to doing this by myself" I said.

We'd been in the space between the boathouse wall and the tall hibiscus for about an hour. Besides the occasional cockroach walking around our feet and a couple of pelicans landing on the dock, there hadn't been any sign of activity.

"I don't think anything is going to happen tonight Matt. Maybe Tobias was the reason for the Thursday night activity. With him dead, whatever was going on may have stopped".

I was about to agree with Dave and suggest we pack it in, when we both heard a car pulling up into the parking spaces.

A lone figure got out of the car and took the time to look around the area very carefully. After seemingly satisfied no one else was in the area the person began walking towards the dock. Getting closer we could see it was a woman. No briefcase, no bag, nothing.

When she got to the dock, she pulled a flashlight out of her coat pocket, turned it on, and flashed some type of signal out into the ocean.

About thirty seconds later, we heard an engine and saw the running lights of a boat start to make its way towards the inlet. It had been positioned about a quarter mile offshore from the club's jetty entrance.

Dave had turned on my night visions and was looking at the woman who had arrived.

"Matt, you're not going to believe who she is. Look!"

As I looked into the binoculars and focused them in on the woman, my jaw opened and dropped wide.

It was Bethany Underwood! What was she doing here? How did she know about this place?

Dave and I exchanged glances to each other with disbelief.

While she waited on the arrival of the boat, Bethany lit up a cigarette and paced the dock. As the boat approached, she tossed her cigarette out into the water and put her hands on her hips as if disgusted it was taking so long to dock the boat.

As the boat came to the dock, a woman came out of the cabin area and grabbed a rope in her hand that had been lying on the back of the boat. She jumped off the boat, oblivious to Bethany standing on the dock, as she tied off the back end of the boat to a cleat. Then she walked briskly to the front of the boat, grabbed a rope from the dock and tied off the front end of the boat. Only after she secured the boat did she walk back to where Bethany was standing.

The boats engines and running lights were now turned off and for a few moments the only sound heard was the gentle ripple of the water against the boat.

Another woman, who obviously had been piloting the boat, stepped up onto the dock holding on to a briefcase.

Dave and I were positioned about forty feet away from the dock. A short exchange of words and some discussions between the women could be heard by us. But nothing was clear to us. All we could hear was bits and pieces.

All the sudden we saw Bethany launch a wicked right cross and slap the crap out of the women's face. The unexpected hit threw the woman way off balance and she fell hard onto the dock.

Then Bethany screamed at the women saying," Don't ever again decide to give my cash away for any so-called goodwill, you sluts. This is my operation and always has been. That idiot husband of mine is dead, and so is the easy way you've done things. Do you understand?"

She continued, "Tobias isn't here anymore to take you shopping for designer shoes, handbags and dresses. From now on, you buy your own shit. No more sugar daddy! Got it? Your job is to have sex with the clients and for that you get paid well. As agreed, Now get my boat back to the marina, clean it up and make sure The Starlight's ready for the second team and their clients on Saturday night. And tell them I'll be here Sunday night, waiting for them and my money."

Dave and I looked at each other with total amazement.

Was the socially and respectable Bethany Underwood of Boca Raton society running a high-end brothel? And is she using the yacht for the activities?

And such a nice name for a yacht, "Starlight". Too bad it's being used for prostitution.

We stayed in position hiding as we watched the women untie the yacht and leave. Bethany walked away from the dock towards her car holding onto the briefcase rather close to her body. When she got to her car, she opened the trunk and placed the case into it. She slammed the trunk lid down making sure it was closed and then got into her car.

Dave and I knew we couldn't follow her because our cars were too far away. But I did have an idea.

Chapter 38

As we walked back to our cars, we were talking about what we had just witnessed. Respectable and socially refined Bethany Underwood and her dead husband Tobias were running a high-class prostitution ring.

"Dave, Bertie called me from her cell phone today. I'm going to call her right now and see if Bethany goes right home. We need to see what's in that briefcase," I said.

"Matt, if it's cash, all I can do right now is to link the money to a prostitution operation. I don't see any other pieces for the murder yet." He continued, "Unless we can link someone to knowing about the cash drops on Thursday nights."

"Dave, remember when we discussed Don from Underwoods office? What if Don knows about this illicit business that Bethany's running? He'd be the perfect person to know about the Thursday night drops and could have been the guy that murdered Tobias – for the cash," I said.

We agreed I would call Bertie right now before Bethany got home if that's where she went. Bertie's phone rang several times and a tired sounding Bertie answered.

"Mr. Matt, why you calling me so late? 'she asked.

"Bertie, Lt. Hahn and I need two favors from you. First, we need to know if Bethany comes home in the next few minutes and if she brings a briefcase into the den. Can you make an excuse and stay up and see her come in?" I asked.

"Sure Mr. Matt, I'll just say I heard her car come in the garage and wanted to see if she needed anything, "she said.

"Thanks, and the second favor I need is for you to call me as soon as she leaves the house in the morning. Can you do that for me Bertie?" I asked.

"Sure, Mr. Matt, does this have something to do with Mr. Underwood's murder? Cause if it does, I want to help you. He was a real nice man to me" she said.

"Bertie, your help may just solve this murder and some other crimes as well. I'll wait to hear from you in the morning," I told her.

Dave overheard the conversation with Bertie but reminded me that none of this was going to be admissible in court. And all we had right now was a Madam running a whorehouse on a yacht.

Chapter 39

Dave and I left each other about midnight exchanging ideas and theories on what to do next. Dave reminded me that we had information on a prostitution business, but the drug running activity was still at large.

The next morning, I woke up around 730 thinking about last night's activity. I went downstairs and saw Winston standing straight up at the counter, reading the morning newspaper.

"Winston, have you ever thought of reading the paper sitting down?" I asked.

"Sire, you stay more alert to your surroundings and concentrate more when standing," he replied.

I told Winston about last night – especially the physical outburst from Bethany towards one of her "girls".

"Sir, my experience has been when someone maintains that amount of controlled decorum and keeping up a pretense of refined calmness, then unleashes physicality in an uncontrolled and unexpected fit of rage, you need to be very careful in dealing with that person."

Winston was right. In the five years knowing the Underwoods, I never would have imagined an outburst like I saw Bethany demonstrate last night.

About 9:30 in the morning, my cellphone rang. It was Bertie calling.

"Hello Bertie, how are you this morning? Anything to tell me?" I asked.

"Mr. Matt, Mrs. Underwood just left the house, she told me she has to go right to the bank and then to Mr. Underwood's Yacht office." She continued," And when she come home last night, I came down to see if she needed anything. She was putting one of them briefcases in the den and told me to go back to bed."

"Great Bertie, that's a big help, thank you."

"If you need anything else Mr. Matt, you let me know" she said.

I decided to call Dave and tell him what Bertie reported. Nothing that we didn't expect, but I also decided not to tell Dave I was going to go to Underwoods office. I wanted to confirm a couple of thoughts I had.

I quickly got dressed and drove down to Underwoods office quickly, in the hopes of beating Bethany there. When I got there, Donna the receptionist was outside on the walkway smoking a cigarette. She saw me pull into one of the Yacht Office Reserved parking spaces and recognized me from our past meetings.

I wasn't sure if Donna was in on this, so I decided to play somewhat stupid.

That's easy for me to do at times.

"Hi Donna, enjoying a little sunshine this morning," I asked her.

She started to take that final drag, the one just before someone throws it away, when I interrupted her and said," Donna, don't throw it away, enjoy your break."

"Thanks," she said.

"Donna, I saw a nice-looking yacht the other day, named 'Starlight'. Is that one of your boats?' I asked.

"No, but we sold the yacht that became the 'Starlight' a couple of months ago to a consulting company" she continued." Don sold the yacht and after the company registered the name, they contacted us to put it on the paperwork," she said.

"Would you mind telling me the name of the company? I liked the boat and thought I would complement them on the purchase," I said.

Donna took the last drag of the cigarette and we walked upstairs into the office. She went over to the file cabinet and pulled out the file with the ownership and warranty papers.

"Trinity ICAM, Ltd. is their name. Here's their phone number as well if you want to call them. I never have talked to them, Don handles everything for them, per the instructions of Mr. Underwood," she continued. "Funny you ask about that boat. Mr. Underwood was always very, very insistent that only Don would talk with them or handle any issues. I never met anyone from that company or talked with anybody. Just Don. And they never wanted their picture on our wall of customers either."

Funny wasn't the word I was thinking about when Don walked in.

"Who never wanted their picture on our wall?' he asked.

Donna responded, "Mr. Tucker was just asking about the yacht, 'Starlight' and I told him you were the only one that handled that company and their boat," she said.

Don was walking right towards me when he burst out with, "Damn right I do, and why the hell do you want to know about the 'Starlight'? It's none of your damn business who our clients are!"

This situation was going to get confrontational quick unless I diffused it.

"Don, I was thinking about Henry's boat the other day and was coming to see you for some more information, because I'm thinking of buying one like his, from you. I told Donna I saw the

'Starlight' on the water the other day and thought it was a very pretty boat. She simply told me you guys sold it and that you personally handle the client, that's all. It's a pretty yacht. It's out of my price range, but a pretty boat. She told me if I buy a boat from you my picture will be on the wall, kinda neat, huh?" I spoke.

That seemed to calm him down and his body seemed to relax.

Donna seemed to relax, and I seemed to have covered the situation.

Just then, Bethany walked into the office.

"Matt why are you here?" she asked.

Slick Don decided to answer for me in a real sarcastic tone.

"Your family friend here, Matt, was asking about the 'Starlight'. I told him our clients are private and when they purchase a yacht, they prefer to keep things private. I told him it's none of his business who buys a boat." Don said.

"Bethany", I said, "I came down here asking about information on a boat like Henry Kane's. I saw the 'Starlight' cruising and thought it was a pretty boat. That's all. I'm afraid Don got a little too protective."

Well, there you go – everyone's happy and calm again, right? Thought so until Bethany surprised me.

"Matt, let me tell you something and let me make it real clear to you. I never have liked you. You always seem to be helping people and being a goodie two shoes. I don't know where you get your money but go buy a boat from someone else. We don't want your business. And we want you to stay the hell out of ours as well."

Well so much for everyone staying calm. This might be fun to push some buttons and see if someone may say too much so I responded with, ...

" Bethany, not a great ales attitude for a yacht brokerage, telling people you don't want their business. Do you think Tobias would have said that?' I asked.

"Tobias was damn fool," said Don.

"Really Don, that's a strange sentiment coming from a guy who worked for him. I thought he treated you well."

"He spent money the wrong way. Bethany and I know how to make real cash money in this business. Tobias never really agreed with us."

Us? I turned to Bethany who was clearly getting upset with Don.

"Really Bethany? You and Don know more about running this business than Tobias did?

I always thought Tobias was a smart businessman and provided you with a lot of nice things. Why it seemed he even was willing to work late into the nights. I mean after all, he was killed late at night working, With Tobias dead, I thought his business may suffer and Don may be out of a job" I said.

"There will be no financial suffering despite my husband's death. Contingent plans were made just like any couple owning a business and we prepared for this," she said.

"Yeah, things are covered so butt out of our business. Bethany and I can handle things without Tobias around!" Don blurted out." And you don't need to come around here no more. Go buy a boat from someone else,' he said.

"Well, I can see my business is not wanted here, so I'll leave. You two aren't the best with sales and customer relations, but hey, as you say, it's your business and you know what you're doing."

As I turned towards the door, I paused, looked back to them, and said, "I still think the 'Starlight's' a good-looking boat. Maybe I'll run into the owners someday."

And with that, I walked out of the office, down the stairs and into the parking lot.

Chapter 40

Donna had told me about the Starlight's real owners and that Don was the only one that handled the company's affairs. From that I assumed she was not in on this little prostitution venture with Don and Bethany. Still, I was in possession of some new information about a company called Trinity Icam. I was thinking that some basic research was going to show me who the real owners of Trinity were. And I was laying odds that ownership would reveal both Bethany and Don's names.

As I was driving back home, I was thinking about Tobias, his murder, and now a revelation by his wife and employee that he was a "fool". On top of that I was thinking about that day in the Mall with Connie, and we saw those great looking women shopping with Tobias.

It was all coming together, bit by bit.

But I still had to connect Bethany and or Don to the murder of Tobias. And there was still the mystery of henrys boat hours and the possible drug ring.

As I pulled into the driveway my cellphone rang. It was Dave.

"Matt, we just got some news from one of our more reliable CI's - that another shipment of drugs is headed this way tonight. But we have no idea where, when, or how. Only that it's going to be a good-sized shipment".

"Dave, I just left Bethany and Don in the yacht sales office. It was clear to me that between the two of them there could be a motive for murder. But the drug running problem is a little far from my, "things to solve" right now."

"Matt, I just need you to keep your eyes and ears open. I've got two dead people from your club and a drug running operation that mentions a club like yours. Just keep vigilant for any unusual happenings or talk around the place, okay?"

Lt. Dave was under some pressure and I decided this was not the time for levity or share more speculation – regardless of how much I was beginning to dislike Bethany and Don.

Winston was in the laundry area ironing (and starching) some of my shirts when I approached him with the meeting I'd just had with Bethany and Don. I also told him what Lt. Dave had just shared about another shipment of drugs coming in tonight.

"Sir, remember when I told you about Mr. Bennett's boat being used for some petty smuggling? Is it possible one of the club's member boats is being used in a similar fashion?", he asked.

No sooner had Winston finished that statement, and then it all came to me. Henry Kane's boat was being used by someone who didn't know that Henry had put another meter on the boat. And Henrys boat was big and damn fast. Could it be? I needed to call Henry right now because I had an idea.

Chapter 41

I called Henry and asked him if he would meet me down at the club dock where he had his boat moored, it was kind of important and may solve the issue of the engine hour difference.

"Sure Matt, how about 3 pm this afternoon? I was going down anyway to wash off the boat and check on it anyway", he said.

When we met, I asked him to check on both engine meters and write down the numbers. I decided not to tell him about someone using his boat for some possible illegal activity.

He would just worry and fret, so I kept it to myself. But I did tell him I had spoken with the salesman at Tobias's company, Don, who might have an answer for the discrepancy.

"Sure, I know Don", he said. "I bought my boat from him. He taught me how to use it, maintain it and was a big help. In fact, he came up to see me last week just to ask me how it was running and if I was planning on any nighttime outings soon."

"What did you tell him Henry", I asked.

"I told him, I wasn't ready for any nighttime fishing and that most of the time I took the boat out around 9 in the morning and back after lunchtime or early afternoon. He seemed really pleased and told me I was smart not to go out at night until I felt more comfortable with the boat. He told me to call him when I decided to go out at night."

"Did you mention anything to him about the engine hour meter issue?", I asked.

"No, he seemed to be in a hurry after he checked on me. I was going to call him and tell him what I did by adding the additional meter. But I forgot. Now that you reminded me, I need to call him and tell him about the difference."

I had some nefarious thoughts that Don was using his boat. But I didn't want him tipped off yet.

"Henry, I'm going to see Bethany tomorrow at her office, and I'll tell Don about it for you while I'm there. Maybe he has an answer. If so, I'll tell you."

"Great, thanks Matt."

It was getting to be late in the day and I had promised Connie, I'd pick her up after work and we would head over to the beach for a light dinner and cocktails at The Boathouse Restaurant. It's always a great place to go after work and enjoy some shrimp tacos and a drink. Casual, relaxing and a nice view of the water.

I called Connie and she said it was a light day at her vet practice, so 6 would be great.

Chapter 42

As macho guys we always like to pretend we don't remember those tender evenings with someone special. But as time goes on, we find ourselves looking at a television ad, seeing a picture in a magazine, or hearing the name of someone we're involved with and care for.

Hearing "her" name today on the radio while I drove over brought a special date and memory back to me. A memory when I had met this wonderful, attractive, and talented lady veterinarian, Connie. We began going out on some fun dates, but we had been meeting in front of the police station because it was across the street from her office.

I think it was because she wanted to make sure I wasn't a mass murderer and by meeting in front of the police department she knew that would keep me on good behavior! I suspected the later!

A couple of weeks into our dating, it was a Wednesday when I decided to call her up and ask about an early dinner date for tomorrow. Since we both had work the next day, it would have to be an early night.

I was really enjoying her companionship and for the first time I felt I had met someone who, "got me". I just wanted to see her again and not have to wait till Saturday – date night!

Much to my excitement, Connie agreed, and I told her I pick her up, at her house around 6.

When I pulled into her driveway, I noticed two odd things. One; her newspaper was still on the driveway from the morning. I picked it up and was going to give it to her. And item number two; it seemed there were no lights on in the house. Being late spring, it was still dark at 6 and I thought it was a little strange? Was she home? Did she have to work late? My anxiety about a cancelled date night was building.

I knocked on the door and heard Connie ask, "Who is it?"

Answering it was me, she told me to come on in.

Walking into that setting that she had prepared for us has stayed with me. It was the first and only time that ever happened to me. And I'll never forget it.

As I walked into her living room, the lamps were turned down extremely low. On the coffee table in front of her were two candles emitting a soft golden glow of light.

And on the sofa was Connie.

She was lounging against the cushions wearing an incredible royal silver shade of silk pajamas. Wow! I had never seen anything-anyone so sensual before. With her top two buttons on her pajama blouse undone, she was gorgeous with the glow of the candlelight against her face. While I dropped the newspaper and it fell to the floor – there were parts of me that were being to rise!

Standing there in front of her, I was trying to figure out how to position myself so I could see more of what was beneath her blouse!

Slowly, while never taking her eyes off me, she got up from the sofa, and without saying a single word, she took my right hand and led me down the hallway and into her bedroom.

In her bedroom there was a small single candle burning on the nightstand next to her bed. Facing each other in front of her bed, she began to unbutton my shirt and I began to unbutton the rest of her pajama buttons. That night we explored each other bodies with a great deal of passion and tenderness.

I suppose it was too much to hope that scene was going to replay itself tonight.

And sure enough, it would not.

As I pulled up in front, Connie was already waiting for me outside. In jeans, polo shirt with her hair in a ponytail, she met me with a big wave and a kiss on the cheek. Not exactly what I was remembering from months ago, but what the heck!

Chapter 43

As we drove over to the restaurant, I told Connie my thoughts. Still, I only had pieces to what seemed like two puzzles. Murder and Drugs. I was hoping somehow, they would start to fit into a clear picture, but too many loose ends were still at large.

When I told Connie about Bethany and her outburst on the dock the other night, she told me it didn't surprise her?

"Really, after meeting her a couple of times at the club and her society manners-her outburst didn't surprise you? Why?'

"Matt, as women we can sense things. Bethany's clock is wound way too tight. She just waiting for the right time to let go. Now you saw it. And I'd be willing to say she's hit her maid Bertie on occasions. She's dangerous. And now knowing about this prostitution operation, and slapping the woman, I'd really watch yourself around her!"

Connie made a lot of sense, so I decided to ask Bertie, in person, tomorrow, if Bethany ever struck her – or Tobias in anger. And it might be a good idea to ask Bethany's secretary, Donna if she ever experienced the wrath of Bethany.

But still, if I found out Bethany had a bad temper, what did that prove? It still didn't answer anything about the murders or the drug operation.

Connie had early morning surgeries scheduled for tomorrow and she wanted to review the cases tonight. We agreed the best thing was to have an early evening for the dog's welfare. Certainly not mine!

After dinner and a brief stroll on the beach, I dropped Connie off at her place around 8, and to my luck and surprise, she planted one of those great and memorable, "good night kisses" on me. Wow!

Chapter 44

Driving back home I was thinking if someone was going to use Henry's boat, without his knowledge tomorrow night. And if they were, how would I track where it goes. I could hide in the bushes and watch, but I wouldn't know where it was going, or who was using it. I needed a way to track it and maybe follow it like the ground crew of a hot air balloon. I needed a GPS device that would transmit.

But I was going to be short on time to get a GPS and place it in Henry's boat.

My other option would be to try and follow from a distance in a smaller craft and hope not to be seen or heard. I decided on following in a boat.

Only problem was, I didn't own a boat.

But maybe I could follow in a jet ski. I didn't own one of those either. Down from the club, about 2 blocks away they did rent them. Problem solved. I'd rent some small jet ski, follow at a distance, and solve this drug running mystery.

Now the question was whether I should call Lt. Hahn and tell Todd what I was up to or not? I decided not to and subject him to a possible waste of time and professional embarrassment.

When I got in, Winston was waiting for me in the kitchen.

"Sir, did you have a nice evening with Ms. Connie?'

"Yes, we did. Nice dinner, quick walk on the beach and I dropped her off to get ready for some dog surgeries tomorrow."

Then I shared with him about the Bethany outburst with her "ladies of the evening", and my idea of following the possible drug runners at a distance tomorrow night.

Winston was not keen on me following at a distance, but in true Winston mode made some great suggestions.

He told me if I was going to rent a personal watercraft, make sure I get The Yamaha because it boasts the bigger fuel tank with a 13.2-gallon capacity. This gives the Yamaha a range of 92 miles while running at an average speed of 40 miles per hour.

"Seriously Winston, where do you come up with these facts?"

"Sir, that's my job. Ever since you started discussing this mystery, I thought you would get to this point one day. I'm here at your service!"

Some service. What else was he thinking I needed help with?

"Thanks Winston, I appreciate that. We'll talk in the morning, get to bed."

"Yes, sir and goodnight to you as well."

When I got into bed, I thought how lucky I was to have him here. And how lucky the Bennett's were to have him by their side all those years.

Chapter 45

The next morning, I woke up around 630, got on my bike and took a ride down the beach road, A1A.

Going down the street I saw 4 different jet ski rental shops and thought about which one to call when I got back to the house. I needed someone to deliver it to my club dock as soon as possible because I had no tow hitch or trailer. And I needed it for ocean use.

And per Winston's instructions, who had the Yamaha with a 13-gallon tank?

When I got back home about 815 and pulled into the driveway, I realized I was thirsty and hungry. But true to fashion as I walked into the kitchen there was Winston, standing, reading the newspaper.

"Good morning sir, good bike ride?"

" Yes, Winston it was good to ride along the beach and smell the saltwater and get the ol heart pumping, getting ready for the day."

Breakfast was ready for me as usual, fruit, danish, hardboiled egg and some yogurt.

"Winston, I need to call the jet ski rental shops and find the one you mentioned to me last night."

"No need sir, I already called, reserved it, and having it delivered to your club dock at 930 this morning. You'll need to be there to sign for it and your proper identification. And Ms. Connie called to say, "Good morning."

Classic, he thinks of everything, and I genuinely appreciate it.

I called Connie's office to wish her well today and her surgeries, but she was already in the middle of them, so I asked her front desk to tell her I called.

Then, ate breakfast, and decided to ride the bike over to the club. A little more exercise never hurt anyone.

When I pulled into the club, the jet ski truck was just pulling in. I greeted them and showed them where they could drive along the side of the club and put the jet ski in the water.

They had a neat rig where they simply attached some straps, had a small crane attached to the bed of the truck and placed the jet ski in the water. All in a matter of about 15 minutes.

I signed the rental paperwork, waiver of injury, gave them my ID and credit card and got final instruction on how to operate it.

"Hey", said the mechanic, "I'm supposed to ask you if you have ever ridden one of these and do I need to show you how to operate it."

I flew a C 7 aircraft for the government in South America for a while, so I think I could figure out how to use Yamaha Jet Ski – with the 13-gallon tank. I mean it was a key, a throttle, and a steering wheel.

"Why don't you show me, just to be sure, and the biggest question I have was – is it quiet?"

The rental shop mechanic started it up and assured me it was incredibly quiet unless I opened the throttle all the way.

If I could follow at a distance and not be seen or heard was all I wanted.

After the mechanic left, I decided to take it for a test run. I wanted to see how slow or fast it could go. And I wanted to see how low I sat in the water, along with how quiet this thing was.

Took it out into the ocean for about 15 minutes and was satisfied it was quiet at a medium speed. There was a nice size storage compartment where I could bring my night vison binoculars, my 9 mm Smith and Wesson and my cell phone.

The jet ski was navy blue, and I was glad because it wouldn't be easy to see at night.

Was that luck I got that dark color, or was it Winston's planning?

Chapter 46

After I got back to the house from the club, I told Winston my plan. He reminded me to, "Sir, stay far back, watch your back, stay quiet and observe. Don't try to solve this alone with no backup or proof."

"Winston, I agree, this is a fact-finding mission. If I can find out if Henry's boat is being used for drug running, it may solve the murder of Brenda and Tobias as well."

"Very good sir", he replied – his tone was not real convincing.

Lt. Hahn called me about 3 o'clock and told me that all their CI's (confidential informants) were quiet, had nothing to report or were playing it dumb. In any case with no real leads or information, he felt the police needed to wait and see if any action got reported in the next day or so.

I told Todd that I was playing a hunch and might have something for him tomorrow.

"Hey, Matt, no holding out on me. If you got something, tell me. Don't leave me in the dark and don't start taking the law in your own hands!"

"Todd, I'm playing on a wild hunch. If I get you involved and it's a bust, you're going to look like an idiot. Let me go along with this one. I promise, you'll be the first call I make if this turns out to be anything."

Todd wasn't happy, but reluctantly agree and told me to be careful. And to call him as soon as I knew anything. I agreed.

Chapter 47

When Connie has early multiple morning surgeries scheduled on animals, she's usually well drained afterwards and likes to call it an early day. She has her visiting vet intern handle the rest of the day.

I called and told her I'd pick her up for an early casual dinner. Maybe go over for some light Italian at Romano's on the Inter Coastal. They have a great dish we both loves.

Pasta e fagioli, meaning "pasta and beans", a traditional Italian dish. Like many other Italian favorites, including pizza and polenta, the dish started as a peasant dish, being composed of inexpensive ingredients. It is often called pasta fasul (fazool) in the United States.

After she got into the car, I asked, "How did surgery go today?"

"Not totally great. Removed a stomach blockage and a bad tooth in a Golden and that went well", she said.

She continued, "Had to repair an ACL on a police German Shepard that got hurt last week chasing a suspect in an alley, and that went well. But I lost a 14-year-old Scottie with a severe kidney infection. I still cry over losing an animal in surgery regardless of how sick they are and how hopeless it might be when they come into me," she said.

Like Connie, I grew up with dogs, Golden Retrievers, and was always sad when they got old, infirmed, and had to be put down.

Knowing it was not a great day for her, I decided not to share in any detail what I was doing late tonight. I kept nebulous.

Got her mind off the day by asking her if she wanted to go out with Dave and Susan this weekend. Maybe dinner, a movie, and a late-night swim we all enjoyed back at my house.

She thought that would be fun. I'd call Todd, and Connie would call Susan and we'd set it up for this Saturday night.

We talked about the latest movies, argued about which one to go see (action flicks were quickly ruled out) and thoughts on where to go for dinner.

I could tell she was feeling better and decided to share with her it would be an early night for her to rest up from the day (no she's not frail) and I had some generic reconnaissance.

Connie knew me well enough to not let that go by without some basic interrogation.

"Matt does this have anything to do with Bethany and or Henry's boat usage? she asked.

"Yes, just trying to find out who may be using Henry's boat at night and why", I replied.

That was the truth. I just left out the part about possible a drug running operation and the fact I would be tailing someone on a jet ski in the dark – on the ocean.

"Well, be careful, no unnecessary risks, I need you to pay for dinner and the movie on Saturday night" she replied with that raised eyebrow and smirk.

We talked and laughed some more. Got to be about 8 o'clock and I drove her back home.

And yes, I got one of those GREAT "goodnight" kisses. Oh Baby!

Chapter 48

Got home after our date and Winston cleaning my gun, binoculars, changing batteries in the night visions and had the decaf coffee ready. He thinks of everything.

We talked about how I was going to play this. I'd go over to the club and lay low and out of sight until I saw someone approach the docks and Henry's boat. Then when they left, I'd give them some distance in the ocean and follow from behind them. Not sure the thought of taking pictures would do any good – other than to verify what I thought might be going on.

Got over to the dock around 9 and saw Henry's boat was still in its slip. I was about to walk over closer to it when I heard a motorcycle coming up the club's driveway and towards the dock area. I quickly hid in the nearby bushes off to the right side of the dock area and kept real still.

The motorcycle stopped less than 50 feet from me, and the figure got off the cycle and looked around. My heart was pounding with adrenaline and I only hoped no one heard it. I stayed motionless for what seemed 5 minutes, when in fact it was about 1 minute. The figure took off his helmet, strapped it to his handlebars and began walking over to the dock.

Just then I heard a rustle in the bushes next to me. It also caught the attention of the guy and he began to walk over.

Crap – now what?

When he was about 20 yards away, two rabbits sprang out from next to me and ran right in front of him and down the yard area towards the driveway.

Seeing them, it satisfied him, and he went and got into Henry's boat. What I did see was that he reached in his pocket, pulled out a key and started up the boat. While the boat was in a low idle, he quickly undid the ropes on the front and back of the boat and released them from the cleats. He tossed them onto the dock, pushed back and got in the cockpit seat.

With what looked like simple precision, with no effort, he backed the boat out of the slip and began to turn it around. Putting it into Drive, he began towards the opening in the jetty and out towards the ocean.

I let him get out into the ocean before I decided to crank up the jet ski and follow. He was about a hundred yards down when I jumped onto the jet ski, started it up and began to follow – quietly at about a quarter throttle. In the back of my mind, I remembered the mechanic when he dropped off the jet ski. "Yeah, it's a quiet unless you open her up full throttle."

So, I kept a distance and my eyes on our friend who likes to borrow boats at night. But why?

Chapter 49

We'd been out in the ocean for about 10 minutes when all the sudden something strange occurred. Our friend in Henry's boat reduced the speed, turned on all the running lights – including the light over the captain's chair. Then he reached down along the side of the cockpit, pulled out two fishing poles and casted them out into the ocean from the back of the boat. He placed both poles in the rocket launchers above his captain's chair. Then lit a pipe, sat back and was cruising at 5-10 knots?

Really, I am following someone who takes someone else's boat out, late at night just to go fishing. Glad I left Todd out of this. I could just hear him rake me over the coals.

After about 5 more minutes of cruising from about 100 yards behind, I was just about ready to turn around and head back to the club dock.

The Great Mystery Caper solved. *"Man uses boat to fish at night!"*

What a waste of time and money.

But just as I was about to turn back - it all began!

Whoever was on Henry's boat flicked all the lights off and on – just once. I grabbed the night vision binoculars and I saw the man reach for some type of handheld radio. While he was talking, I heard a plane off in the distance. As I looked up into the sky where the plane was, I saw the plane flick their landing lights off and on twice!

I could hear the plane coming closer. As I turned to look at it, I realized I was in the same path of the plane, descending towards Henry's boat. I revved up the engine and began to get away from the direct line of the plane coming towards henrys boat from the stern. I went off 25-50 yards so as not to be seen by the airplane's pilot on his approach.

After about 2 minutes, the plane shut off all lights and was coming up to Henry's boat about 50-100 feet above the water.

Thank goodness for no full moon as I would have been easily spotted.

The plane was on a final – about a quarter of a mile behind the boat when the man in the boat turned off all the lights as well.

As the plane approached, I could see a passenger in the plane open the plane doors.

Then as they approached the boat, out came a bundle, then another, then another. They bounced on the water, then floated to a stop.

And with that – the plane pulled up and continued its southernly course. All the time gaining altitude. After about a minute, its strobe lights were back on as it faded away.

Does not take a rocket scientist to know what was dropped.

Then the guy in Henry's boat, pulled along the side of each bundle, grabbed them with a hook, and threw them in the back of the boat. I could see him cover them quickly.

Then all the lights were turned on, and he sat in the chair, continuing to cruise south.

It all took less than 5 minutes from dropped packages – to pick up out of the water – to continuing to cruise south.

But where was he going?

Damn -a real drug running operation and I'm right in the middle of it. Now I understand the phony façade of a man fishing at night and the use of Henrys boat!

From the beach it looked like any ordinary late-night fisherman. All the lights on the boat were lit up, fishing lines in the rocket launchers, a man smoking a pipe cruising along.

No DEA or anyone to suspect what just occurred. How could you? All you saw was a brightly lit boat, two fishing lines and a guy smoking a pipe heading south, running parallel to the beach.

But where was he going? I thought for sure he'd turn around and head back to the club.

Chapter 50

Never once did the guy in Henry's boat ever go past 15 knots. Really cruising as if he had no cares in the world and was in no hurry.

I followed him for about 30 minutes as he entered the inlet from the ocean in Fort Lauderdale. Then he proceeded north up the intercoastal about a mile and turned into a commercial dock area that seemed to be well lit. I could not go near the place as I would be easily spotted.

As he approached the dock area, and I slowed down to a crawl on the opposite side of the intercoastal about 75 yards back, and off to the side, then the dock lights all went off.

As he tied up to the dock, a van pulled up and three people got out. Two men – who looked like muscle and a young woman. Our "captain "didn't seem to say much to the three of them, but I did see he had some "iron" packed into a holster on his right side.

Hard as I tried, I just could not get a good look at his face. Between the hoodie he had on and the darkness, I just couldn't get a good look.

I adjusted my binocs and saw that he threw the bundles up onto the dock and the two men took them away to the van. But the young lady came over to meet our captain. From about 5 feet away she threw what looked like a light tan bank deposit canvas envelope to the man in the boat.

Holy Cow – it was Tobias and Bethany Underwoods daughter Stephanie! That sweet innocent daughter whose wedding Connie and I had attended just two months before! She's right in the middle of drug smuggling, payoffs and what else?

She turned away, not saying a word. Got into the van and drove off.

Wow! A father murdered – but why? A mother running a yacht brokerage business with a Side Hustle of Prostitution on some of their client's yachts and a mid-30's daughter involved in a drug running operation. I felt like I was investigating Ma Barker and her Family Gang.

In case you do not know, Ma Barker was the matriarch of the Barker-Karpis Gang, whose spree of kidnappings, murderers and bank robberies led to her and its members' violent deaths.

Ma Barker, her four sons – Herman, Lloyd, Arthur, and Fred – and Alvin Karpis, formed the Barker-Karpis Gang in 1931. Barker became a wanted woman. On January 16, 1935, Ma and Fred were shot and killed by FBI agents in Oklawaha, Florida.

No sooner was the van out of sight when out captain undid the ropes, turned the boat around and I assumed he was headed back to our club doc? However, I needed to get off the jet ski and fast. I had moored it on a non-descript dock across the canal from where the activity had just taken place. But I decided to get off the jet ski, lay down and be real still on the dock, not move and hope whoever was in the boat did not even look over my way.

He passed by me but seemed busy counting the money that was in the bag, lighting his pipe and steering the boat towards the intel out to the ocean. All the lights on the boat were on again.

He got into the inlet and was heading out into the ocean – heading north when I began to follow him.

But the same "MO". Cruising with all light on, fishing poles out and sitting in the cockpit smoking his pipe. His speed never got past 15 knots.

After about an hour and half we arrived back at the club's dock. I laid back until our mystery man had docked the boat. Then I came in very quietly but decided not to go all the way to the dock. I would stop on the jetty/inlet and tie off the jet ski to a rock. The worst thing that would happen was the jet ski would rub up against some rocks.

But I really wanted to see if I could see a face of that man was.

He was walking down towards the parking area where he had left his motorcycle. I tried to climb over the rocks and come up the back side of the building next to the parking lot and get a closer look.

He got on his motorcycle and was about to put his helmet on. I knew he would be gone in an instant and I would never see his face. But Lady Luck was on my side!

He started his motorcycle, and instantly I knew and recognized that sound.

That was the same exact engine sound I heard the night Tobias was murdered by the man on the motorcycle.

But greed got the best of him – and a big help for me.

He decided to count his money again before putting on his helmet. That gave me just enough time to get a little closer and focus my night visons onto him. Maybe – just maybe I'd get a good look. As I focused on him, he turned around one more time looking for anyone that might be around, when I saw his face.

The "weasel" himself. Dave – Bethany's salesman, gofer, and all-around shithead.

Now I got it. Bethany running a prostitution ring, her daughter Stephanie's running a drug smuggling operation, and the weasel himself – Dave – in the middle of it all. Murderer, and drug runner.

Now I knew who murdered Tobias. It was Dave. But why?

Chapter 51

After Dave, the Weasel left, I went back and got the rented jet ski and tied it up on the dock. Felt bad about tying it up on the rocks for a few minutes so I overcompensated by using three bumpers to make sure nothing happened,

When I got back home, Winston met me at the door. Connie had left a message with Winston asking me to send her a text when I got in. So, I sent a quick note to her cell telling her I was back home.

I told Winston all that happened and that I was thinking about calling Todd when Winston suggested I wait till morning. "Why ruin his night of sleep?" He was right, so I went up to my room, got a shower to get all the salt and sweat off me and climbed into bed.

No secret that I tossed, turned, and was trying to figure out how to catch them all? And if I did tell Todd everything I had witnessed, what could he do? No witnesses, no pictures, no evidence. Just my description of events. All circumstantial. Finally, about 2 am I drifted off to sleep.

Chapter 52

The next morning, I woke up and began to think about the Underwoods. Bethany was the recipient of a large monthly trust fund and her husband had a successful yacht brokerage. Was that not enough? Stephanie grew up with everything a young lady could want. She was going to inherit her father's business and her mother's trust fund. Was that not enough? And why did Dave murder Tobias? And who murdered Brenda our club waitress and why? Was she somehow involved or connected?

Loose ends bother me. There had to be some connection between all of this.

Todd called me just as I began a second cup of coffee. I asked him to come on over and let me share all I had seen and figured out.

He told me he had a meeting until 10 and would come over then. Until then he told me to write down everything I'd seen so as not to forget anything. Really Todd? Did you forget our mutual backgrounds or were you just reminding me of my age?

In any case, I did grab pencil and paper and wrote down some of the things I saw last night, and the night Tobias was murdered.

As I wrote down what I witnessed I just kept thinking about the Underwoods.

Sure, they had money, possessions and the image of a prominent family that had been blessed. What was it that made them want more? What drives the rich to the point of criminal activity, mayhem, and murder. How much is not enough?

Bethany, Stephanie, and Dave were all involved, firsthand in prostitution, drug running and murder. But why murder Tobias?

After all, Connie and I had seen him in the Galleria Mall that day with two of the "working ladies" and Bethany. No surprise to anyone there!

The biggest surprise was their daughter, Stephanie, and the drugs?

"Hey, Matt, talk to me" was the voice I heard from Todd. Writing in such detail and concentration I never heard the doorbell. Winston let him in just as I was putting down my pencil.

"Todd, have I got some news, details and information for you" I said.

Outlining all that I had seen took about 20 minutes, then another 5 minutes to share my questions with him and what to do next?

Todd was taking notes as well when he finally said," Matt, I'll take it from here and alert my contacts in DEA. We'll open an investigation and see what we can come up with on the drug running and I'll go question Dave and Bethany on Tobias and Branda's murder."

From someone so smart that I admire – that was such a stupid reply to what I just told him.

"Todd, you've got nothing more than some here say from me. DEA is going to laugh at you. At best they'll watch the beach for a run – but so what? They catch Dave running drugs but can't tie him to the murder. You get to question Bethany on prostitution, only if you catch her in the act. And Stephanie gets arrested and charged only if you catch her in the act" I said.

Todd responded with, "at least we interrupt the flow of drugs and try to put the squeeze on Dave for the murders."

"You're putting a band aid on a major cut" I said. There must be a better way!

Later that same day Connie called, and we set a time for dinner that night. I'd tell her all about what happened the night before and who I think murdered Tobias and Brenda.

I picked up Connie at her place about 630 and drove over to O'Reilly on the beach. I told her all that I had witnessed last night as well as questions on why Tobias was murdered by Dave. They were all in it together – so what went wrong to have Tobias killed? And why was Brenda killed? Was there a correlation between the two murders?

I told Connie I was a little mystified.

And then in classic Connie fashion – she had a great thought and a plan! Sometimes I think women make better detectives because they think about things in a different perspective. Not better, not worse – just a different point of view. And now what Connie said made all the sense in the world.

Her outline of the situation between Dave and Bethany was clear. And how she suggested a plan was brilliant.

Dave was running a drug smuggling activity with Bethany's daughter, Stephanie on Wednesday, or Thursday nights only.

And Bethany was running a prostitution ring with high rollers on Friday and or Saturday nights. So, trying to catch them together could be tough since each had their own days of the week for their activities.

But Connie suggested there was one day of the week, they could be together and discuss, compare, or conspire. Fridays

And the where was easy – the Yacht Brokerage Office. Just where I had seen them before and had the run in with Dave.

I knew that if I suggested this to Todd, he would have to pass on it. No way was a judge going to issue a "bug" for the yacht brokerage office based on any of the evidence I had given him.

Connie and I were discussing potential scenarios, none of which seemed like it would solve anything. I suggested we head back to my place, have an Irish Coffee, and keep thinking on this.

So, we left the restaurant and headed back to my house. The night sky was clear, the temp was simply perfect, so I put down the top of the Healy and cruised home with my best girl's hand on my lap.

Chapter 53

We no sooner pulled into the carport on the side of the house when Winston greeted us.

"Miss Connie, so good to see you again. I hope everything is going well at your clinic?"

Connie gave Winston a big hug and a kiss on the cheek and responded with, "Winston, all is well. Thank you for asking. If you ever want to leave this bum, there's always a position for you with me and my staff."

"Thank you, Ms. Connie, I'll keep that in mind," he said with a slight smirk aimed at me.

Winston makes a great Irish Coffee but before I could even ask him, "May I fix you both an Irish Coffee – decaffeinated since it is getting late?"

We agreed and headed for the lounge chairs by the pool. A great place to think at night. The silence of the night, a small breeze that makes that creates that special sound of palm branches moving and the pool lights reflection from the water.

We had been discussing the case for about 15 minutes when Winston came out with the two Irish Coffees in mugs and some strawberries in a light sweet cream.

"Thanks Winston", I said, "you think of everything. Just wish you had the answers on this one."

"Sir?" said Winston.

Connie then outlined very clearly the issues we were facing to Winston. He stood very still while he listened, all the while starring directly at her with great intensity. After she was through, he folded his hands behind his back as if he were in the military – at ease - and looked directly at me.

"Sir, the shortest distance between two points is a straight line."

What?

"Winston, we're trying to figure out the murder of two people, a drug smuggling operation and a high-end prostitution ring and you're talking about geography," I said.

Continuing, I blurted out to him, "What I'd like to do is to help the local PD and DEA solve a couple of items here, not road course geography lesson", I said.

When I glanced over at Connie for some reassurance of what I had just said to Winston, what I got was one of the coldest icy glares a woman could give.

But without a missed beat Winston replied to me in a cool, calmed and collected manner.

"Sir, Ms. Connie has already solved 50% of the case by suggesting all parties probably have a meeting in the brokerage office on Fridays. Fridays, after the narcotics run and prior to the night's prostitution activities. Then likely counting money on Mondays."

While I agreed with Winston, I still did not understand how we could do anything with that information about Mondays.

Then Connie raised her hand and pointed directly at Winston, winked with a smile, and said, "I know what Winston means about the straight line between two points."

Glad someone did because I must admit I was still confused, until…

Chapter 54

Winston brought his arms from the "at ease" position and crossed them over his chest. Remember, this is guy who is 6'4", 285 pounds and a size 50 Long suit. And then he shared the following action to resolution.

"Sir, think about the shock and surprise value of someone confronted them in their office from out of nowhere. Outline how Mrs. Underwood has been followed and her illegal activities are now known. Confront her accomplice, the Don man you describe, along with Stephanie's involvement with drug smuggling and distribution."

Connie jumped in with, "Winston, you are right! They'll be stunned, angry, confused and darn mad they have been caught after thinking they were so smart."

It was only 9:30 pm so we decided to call Todd and ask him to come over.

"Hey jerk face, you want me to come over at this hour and listen to your theories. Matt, I need more", said Todd.

"Todd, really? Its 9:30 pm. I know you watch TV until after the news ends at 11:30. Just come over because we have a plan and we need you to hear it out, give us some guidance and direction and tell us how we can help you solve this. Together we can solve three major crime issues."

Thirty minutes later, I could hear Todd's car in the driveway. One thing about a gravel driveway, you just cannot drive in quietly.

Winston met him at the door and "escorted" him to the pool area where Connie and I were talking.

"Matt, this better be really good with a lot of details I know you've held back on. I'm going to cuss up a storm in front of Connie if it's not," Todd said.

Thank goodness Winston showed up with a tumbler of Bourbon and one ice cube (Winston never forgets anything) for Todd.

"Winston, thank you, this may or may not calm me down, but it's a start."

As we all smiled at Todd's remark, Winston walked away.

We shared everything with Todd. From the look and sound of the motorcycle, the following and surveillance of the drug operation and who was involved. When I told him Underwoods daughter Stephanie was involved, he was shocked. Just five years ago Stephanie was making her Society Debut in Boca Raton.

"Wow, from a Debutante Ball to drug running and distribution operation on a wharf in less than 5 years," said Todd. "Guess it never amazes me, that no matter how much privilege and money some people have, they just have to have more – even if it's illegal," said Todd.

Connie and I finished sharing all the final details, and so much more I had not shared with Todd before, like my thoughts on the murder of Brenda the club waitress and Tobias Underwood. And all the details with Bethany's "Ladies of the evening" business, Todd shifted in his chair.

Staring out at the pool he said, "Matt, I really wish you had told me all of this before now. I guess what I can do now is to go arrest them all and convince one of them to cut a deal by ratting out the others."

"Lousy idea Todd," I said. "All you'll do is bring them in, they go quiet, lawyer up on you and probably bond out on an arraignment. Too much power, prestige, and money. There's only one other way I know."

Connie glanced over at me with a "don't even think about it" look.

"Look Todd, I'm willing to wear wire. Don hates me, and Bethany does not think much of me. If I go in unexpected, start a discussion I can get them to confess. Especially since I have followed each of their activity and know the details. They will deny everything at first, but I will keep pushing until someone blurts out. Then the rest will clamor for everyone to shut up. I'll tell them they can turn themselves in or I'll go to the police."

"No way", said Connie, "this is something for Todd and an undercover officer to handle – not you. Or Todd can try to get one of Bethany's working girls to flip on them."

"Connie's right," said Todd. "You're too close, and if Don is a killer, he may decide to take you out right there. I can't protect you and I won't ask you to do this", said Todd.

"Guess what everyone, I'm not asking, I'm telling you. This is the only way. I'm the one that can agitate them into confession while wearing the wire. Just make sure, you're close by when the fireworks of emotion and confessions are blurted out."

"Matt, seriously, you've now found out, firsthand, these are dangerous criminals. They are going to be banded together for survival. Who knows who will explode first and what they will do? There's a good chance each of them is armed and it's anybody's guess who might get ticked off and pull out a gun," said Todd.

"I know, I've got a plan to start and finish it fast — and without me getting shot", I said.

Chapter 55

It was about 11:00 pm when I called it a night.

"Todd, drive home safely and watch the news. We'll talk tomorrow", I said.

Connie decided to spend the night. "If you take me home, I'll just toss and turn all night thinking about this. If I am not going to sleep, I may as well not sleep here with you", she said. "Besides, maybe I can talk you out of this plan of yours."

Such warmth!

Winston was in the kitchen as we said goodnight. He didn't say much, but had that serious, look of problem solving on his face as he said goodnight to us.

Connie and I took showers and climbed into bed. I was mentally tired and thought I could fall asleep quickly. But!

Connie sat up in bed and turned to me. "Matt, I love you and don't want you to get hurt – or killed. Is there anything I can do or say to talk you out of this plan? Really, there must be another way", she said.

"There's no other way. I know I can get them to confess and wearing a wire will allow Todd and his team to get a great confession. The edge I have is that they don't like me, and I can use that to my advantage. They'll respond on emotions, but I'll be keeping calm knowing what I need them to say", I said.

Connie looked into my eyes, grabbed my neck, pulled me close to her. And while a gentleman does not kiss and tell, we had a genuinely nice evening in each other's embrace.

The next morning, we woke up, got dressed and headed downstairs.

True to form, Winston had already made Connie's favorite coffee with fresh ground beans, strawberry yogurt, blueberries, and a banana nut muffin.

"I trust you all slept well? asked Winston.

"He slept; I worried all night Winston", said Connie. "And thank you for breakfast. I appreciate it, especially the coffee, thank you again. And as a side note, after Matt comes back from dropping me off, have him explain his idiotic idea. And help him see the danger in it and why it should be someone else, please! If anyone can talk some sense into him, it's you Winston," said Connie.

I decided to keep quiet. In certain situations, I only look stupid. I knew better than to start a debate with her first thing in the morning. Especially after such a nice physical evening.

I grabbed the keys to the Healy, and we headed out to the car. Walking hand in hand to the garage across the gravel driveway, not saying anything but listening to the sound of footsteps in the gravel. I knew what she was thinking and wishing for. And I suspect she knew how committed I was to be solving this series of crimes.

The morning Florida sun was already out, and its rays felt good. With the top down, not much was discussed as we turned on the radio as I drove Connie to her condo.

When we got there, I jumped out and opened her door. Two reasons, one is that I am a gentleman, the other is the passenger door handle doesn't work from the inside.

Got to remember to get that handle fixed when this is all over. Unless I am dead.

"See you later tonight for dinner my dear Dr. Connie", I said.

"Matt, thank you for a nice evening of worry mixed with pleasure. All I ask is that you talk this over with Winston this morning when you get back. Then at least meet with Todd and think hard about their thoughts on your involvement. I love you", she said as she walked away.

"I promise I'll talk with Winston as soon as I get back home, and to call Todd in the morning, "I yelled back.

"Call me later after lunch, I have a couple of minor surgeries to handle before lunch," she said.

And with that, I headed back home. Not really wanting to explain this to Winston, but a promise is a promise. And besides, I really did value Winston's advice despite my background and history.

Chapter 56

The plan took some time to explain to Winston. As I shared how I felt the situation needed to be handled, he just stood there staring and stroking his beard. Finally, when I was all through explaining he looked at me and simply said, "I think it's a good plan, but prepared for emotional flare ups and someone pulling out a weapon in rage."

He remarked that Lt. Todd Hahn better be close by with backup staff- both tactical and technical. And to make sure that the wire was functioning perfectly. In addition, he reminded me it was going to be necessary to carry a gun myself because the situation was going to get out of hand quick. When we finished talking, he agreed that unfortunately I was the best person for the task, because of their dislike for me. I could use their emotions to my advantage. Plus, I knew all the details of each of the three crimes being committed.

Todd was out of the office and I was told he was in court, back in the afternoon. So, I went into my den with a tablet and pen to outline what items and actions needed to be done next.

First, I had to make sure I had a current trip of Don's (the weasel) drug run, so I had him and Stephanie being photographed, no matter how lousy a night vision photo was going to turn out.

Secondly, I had to make sure Bethany had a coordinating night out scheduled on the "Love Boat". If I could get all these events within 2-3 days of each other, I stood a great chance of them all meeting together on a Monday morning in the office to handle the cash payments and the drug distribution details.

Finally, I had to make sure I knew the office layout in case I needed to duck and run when the guns started to go off – in my direction. I had to have my physical plan worked out in advance. Which one of the three would pull a gun on me first? Stephanie, Bethany, or Don? I had to think about that detail. It was my life after all.

It was lunch time on a Wednesday which meant there was a good chance Don would make the run tomorrow night. Lately, each drug run had been on a Thursday night, so I figured I was going to need the jet ski one more time.

Winston planned for the jet ski rental and it was delivered to the club dock that afternoon. I went over late in the day and took it out of the inlet and into the ocean. I wanted to make sure about two items. One, make sure it was a quiet running jet ski. And two, it was a dark color. Turns out the jet ski they delivered was the same brand that I had used before. Quiet and navy blue.

Over the last two weeks I had stopped by the pier that Bethany and her girls used on Friday and Saturday nights to drop off the "johns". No real surveillance, just checking to see if they were still using the same place for off-loading. They were. Bethany seemed to be constant in her methodology.

Men came aboard at the yacht at a dock location north of the brokerage office. They would cruise for 3 hours and drop everyone back at the same pier. The "johns" left the yacht first and after a while, the girls left. Plus, the fact, it was well lighted area, so some additional pictures would be easy to obtain of men leaving the yacht, girls in Bathrobes (or less) saying goodbye. Getting film of them and their car license plates would help later if we went to trial. Guys like this will "roll over" quick to stay out of the public press. And finally, we would want to get shots of The Queen herself – Bethany sending the men and girls off into the night.

The girls all had their BMW's, Vettes and Jags parked there. It was easy for me to have all the license plate numbers of their cars for the future.

So, my plan was now in place.

One, follow Don tomorrow night and get some more details and pictures.

Two, follow Bethany this Saturday night and get some more details and pictures.

Three – be prepared to hang out at the yacht brokerage parking lot on Monday morning until I saw everyone arrive.

Finally, and the big one - approach them all at the same time in their office. Sounded good, but I knew two of the three (Don and

Bethany) where real hotheads and I needed to plan for an outburst from them or worse.

Chapter 57

Todd returned my call later in the day and I asked him if I could stop by the office and share some thoughts and details with him. He agreed and we set a time for 4 pm. I picked 4 pm because it tends to be the slow time of the day and I thought I would have his attention just a little better.

When I arrived, the station was busier than I planned, and we ended up meeting in one of the interrogation rooms. That was a little strange knowing anyone could be looking at us in the room with the one-way mirror.

Todd laughed at that and said no one was in there and not to worry. Only when I had handcuffs on, be on his bad sine and have been caught doing something illegal would I need to think about everything being recorded. Great!

In any case I opened with my plan to Todd. He listened intently and took down a lot of notes. For the first time in a long time, he did not interrupt, just patiently listened, and took notes. All the while, I kept looking into the mirror as if I were going to see anyone besides us. When I was through, Todd put his pencil down. Pushed away the pad and looked at me.

"Matt, everything you say makes sense. I cannot argue with the plan. But there are a couple of glaring items that make me worry. One, you are not law enforcement of any kind anymore, and I'm going to get some heat on your involvement from my superiors. Then we need to go to the District Attorney in getting you wired and micd up", he said.

He continued," Remember, Susan is the Assistant District Attorney and she's going to be really skeptical of how we're handling this. If this whole mess blows up, we're all losing our jobs."

"Todd, we've been friends for a long time and have worked on several cases together, I know my place, but this is three serious crimes," I said.

He interrupted and again with, "Secondly, if they suspect you're wearing a wire, they'll never confess anything and all your work and my efforts with you are going to go up in smoke, right there."

Before I could reply, he leaned over to me and said, "finally, if this gets out of hand, and it will, I probably can't get to you in time after they confess, and someone pulls out a gun. They will shoot you dead on the spot and figure out some story. You threatened them, it was self-defense, or you were offering them a plan and threatened them if they didn't go along with you."

He continued with, "we've been close friends for some time. I do not want anything to happen to you. You can't wear a vest; you might get searched for a wire and you might just end up dead."

"Todd, I like living and I don't want to be dead either. But we have got a major trio of crimes going on, and you and I can end it. I need you to get on board with me.

You have been with me on two occasions seeing Bethany's operation. I think there's more to it, but I can't prove anything else. But I have some suspicions. Now, let's do the surveillance one more time together on all three activities. The drug run, the hand off and distribution group and the prostitution activity" I said.

He saw and knew I was not going to let this go and I was going to be involved. So, we went to the next level of planning.

Todd would alert the Coast Guard and DEA about the drug drop. But they were only to photograph and chase the plane, after Don had picked up the packages in the ocean and the plane was on its way back to wherever it came from. Todd and I would be in jet skis together, following Don at a distance that would allow for photographing with telephoto lenses and time/date stamps for evidence submitted later.

Todd got approval for the technical surveillance at the dock where Stephani and her goons picked up the drugs from Don. In advance, they would have people standing by with cameras and recorders. They would install them under the disguise as local electrical utility workers so as not to arise any suspicion. But under no circumstances, were they to make an arrest, until after we got them to confess on the following Monday. Hopefully.

Todd and a technician would be with me as we photographed the prostitution ring, the "johns" leaving the yacht in their cars and the "girls" driving away in their cars.

The last item we needed to finalize was, "the wire" and how we would handle that. We both suspected that someone might think I was wearing one, pull a gun on me and search. Finding one would not go well for me, or the operation. I thought Don was too stupid, and Stephanie might be too much of a rookie at crime to think about asking or thinking about it. But Bethany was smart, cunning and I suspected well prepared for something like this. She'd be the one to bring it up.

The technical team showed me a variety of devices. But all of them seemed a little too obvious. Between wires, transmitters, and earpieces I just did not like any of them. Nor did I trust the fact they could easily be concealed.

I told the technical team to let me think it over. Todd and I finished plans for tomorrow night's run, and I left for home.

Chapter 58

Driving home it all seemed to fit except for the wire issue Thinking about the need to get the confessions transmitted seemed like a hurdle that might be too difficult to solve. And without clearly received transmissions, anything with breaks in them, would be inadmissible in court.

I mentioned it to Winston as well, telling him the options the technical team at the police station offered and how none of them seemed like they would work, without being discovered.

To my surprise he offered up," Sir, if allow me to make a call, I think I can offer some options that would be acceptable to you."

"Sure, go ahead," I said. Not really knowing what he might come up with.

It was about 6:30 and had made a dinner date with Connie. I was going to have to tell her about my conversation with Todd, and Winston. But the worst part was that our mutual friend, and her close friend Susan, the ADA was also going to be involved.

I jumped into the pool for a quick three laps to clear my mind, went upstairs, showered, shaved (too close and nicked my nose), changed clothes and headed out to the garage.

Just then, I heard a car coming into the driveway and from the sound of the gravel it was moving fast. I turned to look out to see who it was.

It was Bertie! Bethany and Tobias's housekeeper. She saw me and waved my way, but I could tell it was a wave of concern. She jumped out of her car, almost as soon as it stopped and slid a little bit on the gravel.

"Mr. Matt!" she yelled. "Ms. Bethany is making some big plans for Saturday night", she said. "I overheard her talking on the phone to someone and she said she needed more money to buy more goods. I think she was talking about drugs."

"Bertie," I said, "Did she talk to anyone else?"

"Yes, two men, they come to the house and go meet with her in Mr. Tobias old den room. The she tells me to go into the kitchen and leave them alone. Then I hear the men tell her, they will get some more money also to buy more product."

"Great Bertie, this is big help. You did good," I said. "Now go back and let me know if any other news or meetings take place.

But do not call me, just come by at the end of the day when you leave on Friday for the weekend, okay?"

"Okay, Mr., Matt, be careful, that strange man Mr. Don, he comes by sometimes and they fight and argue about what to do next. I do not like him. He is a strange and dangerous man I think."

Bertie left and I got into my car. Pulled out my cell phone and called Todd before I left the property.

"Hey, Todd, its Matt. Remember Bertie, the Underwoods housekeeper? Well, she just came by and told me there have been men coming into the house and telephone calls. She's overheard them talking about the need for more money to buy more product. I think this Thursday and Saturday night could be really interesting."

"Matt, keep her out of this. I'm worried as an informal CI (Confidential Informant) she could get caught up in this and be done away with," he said.

"Let's talk some more about this tomorrow. I have a dinner date with Connie."

"Really? Did you forget all four of us are meeting tonight at 7:30 over at The Fine Diner?"

I had forgotten we all set up a dinner date for tonight. Me, Connie, Todd, and Susan. This was going to be a delicate, if not difficult dinner for all of us.

"I did forget, see you in about 30 minutes at the Fine Diner. Let's hope this goes well with the girls tonight."

Chapter 59

Of course, when we all got to the restaurant, there was no wait. Which meant they seated immediately. Besides the usual greeting, hugs, and kisses there was a tense atmosphere in the air.

The waiter came by, introduced himself, (I really don't need to know their names) and asked if we wanted something to drink.

Connie was first with a "gin martini, dry, I'm going to need it. Susan jumped in with, "make that two of them, I agree with her." Todd ordered a draft beer, and I ordered a glass of merlot with the remark of, "I'll add some finesse and charm to this dinner."

There were 3 sets of eyes looking at me – and not with love and affection.

"okay, let's get this out on the table and go from there" I started.

"Look everyone, there's been two murders, a drug ring operating out of the club and a prostitution ring that may have some more details to it. You all know I have been following this and have the evidence. Some of it is solid and some is only statements from me. But I have a plan to end it all, once and for all."

Todd jumped in with, "Look, I don't like having Matt involved, but I have to agree. With this group, he is the best person to pull this off. He is a big boy, knows what is at risk and is willing to help. Not much more I can do or say to convince him to back off. And at this point instead of fighting with him the best thing I can do is to support him and back him up with the necessary technology and people."

Connie has been quiet all too long and finally opened up with, "I still don't understand why Matt has to be the one. Why not use an undercover person, or call in the Feds and turn all the evidence, photos anything else you have over to them? Why does Matt have to be the Knight coming in on the galloping horse? It's dangerous and he can get killed! For what? Breaking up a drug ring and eliminating some prostitution?

Somebody else will just replace that activity. It won't stop because you put a dent in someone operation!"

What happened next surprised Todd, Connie, and me. No sooner had Connie finished and there was a moment of silence. Then, Susan, the Assistant District Attorney (and Todd's main squeeze) spoke in words I would never have thought of saying.

" Look, I don't like any of this. But I swore an oath as an assistant district attorney to uphold the law and prosecute criminals. No matter how minor or major the crimes. That is my job. Sometimes it's difficult. This is one of those times. We are close friends and professional colleagues; I know Todd feels the same way. He took an oath as well to uphold the law and to arrest and prosecute criminals and criminal activity. Connie, you also took an oath as a veterinarian. To eliminate pain and suffering in all animals. All God's creatures, big and small."

There was silence as the drinks came and were served. No one said anything. Then Connie of all people, raided her glass and said, "okay, here's a toast to a successful operation. Susan, if anything happens to either of these guys, I'll never talk to you again. Todd, if you let anything happen to my Matt, I will kill you. And Matt, be careful because of you get hurt or worse, I will never forgive you."

There was what appeared to be an immediate release of tension in the air. Almost as if everybody agreed to what was going to take place over the next five days.

Todd jumped in with, "Connie, I have never liked the idea of Matt being in the center of this. I have thought of every other scenario I would prefer. Using someone in our office, using an undercover officer, even me getting involved. I just can't come up with one, "he said.

"And I do agree with you, we could easily turn everything over to the Feds. But knowing how they operate; it could be months before they put a stop to this. And how many more people may needlessly get killed, like an innocent club waitress Brenda and even Tobias himself?'

Believe it or not, I decided not to say anything. And I just let the conversation go on with some of the details, remarks and opinions going on and on, somehow, talking about it, seemed to make it less stressful.

Talking about Thursday nights plan and getting the Coast Guard and DEA included and then discussing Saturday nights surveillance seemed somewhat harmless. These are the details they were all talking about.

And while everybody seemed to be getting more acceptance to the action plan, I kept thinking of how best to start the entire confrontation in the yacht brokerage office on Monday. And not get killed.

Dinner was over and we decided to go back to my house for a night cap. I called Winston and told him the four of us would be coming back and sitting by the pool. He appreciated the call and responded in his normal manner responded with, "Sir, I'll have refreshments prepared for you, Lt. Todd and the ladies. Carefully drive sir, and I will see you when you arrive."

Classic Winston, as we pulled into the driveway, Winston was standing in the doorway, arms folded, waiting on us like a parent waiting for their teenager to come home from a date.

As we all approached the front door, Winston took a step back, unfolded him arms, crossed his hands on his chest and said, "Ladies, Ms. Connie, Ms. Susan, so genuinely nice to see you both again. As usual you're both looking attractive, making me wish I were 30 years younger."

"Please take yourselves to the pool area. I have the towels on the chairs by the side of the pool should you decide to put your feet into the water, Winston said.

"Refreshments will be brought to you shortly; I've prepared a little something for you all."

Okay, guess I'm not needed for anything – Winston has it all covered.

We all went and sat by the pool. The girls did side on the side and dangle their legs in the water making ripples that reflected to pool lights in a sparkling manner.

About Ten minutes later, Winston came out with a tray. Fresh brewed coffee done in a French Press, cream, sugar, and an assortment of small pastries?

Where does he get these at the last moment?

"I have prepared decaf coffee so no one stays up too late, it is a working night and some refreshments for you. I know you all will need to be at your work tomorrow. Please let me know if you need anything else."

I was not sure, but I think "dad" just told us not to stay up too late?

As he began to walk away, Connie asked, "Winston, would you be willing to hear the plan these three have in mind for solving the crimes Matt's been following with Todd? I'd like you to know what they are planning and get your thoughts on it?"

Funny thing, Todd did not seem to mind sharing with Winston his thoughts on this caper. Neither did Susan on discussing the wire, entrapment and getting the confession on tape. And of course, Connie was eager to share why she thought I should not be involved and why this was a bad idea.

Winston stood tall and almost at attention the whole time. Occasionally stroking his beard. And then said the following.

"I agree with you Ms. Connie, I do wish there were someone else. There is not. I agree with Lt. Todd Hahn that getting the Federal authorities involved would be a waste of time. And yes, Ms. Susan, I know there will be a fine line to make sure all the evidence is legal and admissible. Finally, as you know, I have a great fondness for Mr. Matt and would never want or allow anything to happen to him. I also owe my life to him. He came to my aid when some would have walked by. And Mr. Matt, I know you, your past and your skills. So, I trust between all of you, there will be a good outcome." And with that, he excused himself and walked, slowly back into the house.

It was about 11:00 o clock when we decided the night should end. Todd drove Susan home and I drove Connie back to her house as well.

Not much was said in the car, but you could hear all the gears grinding in Connie's head.

When we arrived at her place, she turned to me and said, "Look, I know that no matter what I say, you are going to do this anyway. Please be careful and ask for help if needed." And then she added, "so get your butt out of the car, open my door so I can go get some sleep. And when this is over – get the darn doorknob fixed!"

"Yes, ma'am", I replied.

I walked her to her door to say goodnight. When we got to the door, she reached in her purse, got her keys, and turned to me.

"Here!" And I got a great kiss good night. The one where her hands are on my neck!

Chapter 60

When I got back to the house Winston was up (as usual) waiting for me in his normal spot. Kitchen counter, reading the newspaper, acting like nothing was unusual about his being up and waiting for me.

"Good evening sir, I trust Ms. Connie got home safely?"

"Yes, not happy about this, but I think she knows how I feel about it. All I can say is that we agree to disagree."

"Sir, I've taken the liberty to OUTLINE some of the items you'll need to do as soon as possible. Many of them I can prepare in advance for you and Lt. Hahn."

"Thanks Winston, I'll take this with me upstairs, read it over and see you in the morning. Thanks for the support this evening, I appreciated it."

With that, I did an about face and headed up to my room. I washed my face, put on some sleeping shorts and top and climbed in bed. I was all prepared to read over Winston's outline, but my eyes were too heavy, and I was reading the last of a sweet good night message on my cell phone from Connie. The reading would have to wait until morning.

Chapter 61

The next morning Todd called while I was having breakfast.

"Matt, I've gone out on a limb and assembled an action plan with support from my end. I'll come over in about an hour with Ted Lightmiller from the DEA as well."

Finished breakfast, took a quick shower, and had read over Winston's outline. It was divided into two sections. The first section was the Action Plan and Personnel. The second section was on items needed. Items like night vision cameras with telephoto lenses, long range hearing devices, jet skis and some suggested weapons.

This was complete and covered some items I had not thought of. Thanks Winston!

Todd drove up with Lightmiller. I had met him and worked with him briefly on another situation last year. Ted was a By the Books DEA Agent in Charge. While there were times, I thought he took too long – he was thorough, complete, and trustworthy. I did not mind he was here and involved.

We went out to the pool area and sat down. Winston came over with coffee, juice, and fruit.

"Good morning Lt. Hahn." Said Winston. "Hello to you Mr. Lightmiller", said Winston and he left us. I could see Lightmiller was a little intimidated. Winston was 6'3", 275 pounds, broad shoulders, and the pirate patch over his eye.

Lightmiller was about 5'7", small frame man! Get the point?

"Matt", started Ted, "Todd's told me what you have. This could be tricky to put together in the way you want to do it. I would like to suggest we wait about 2-3 weeks and get some more evidence and get some more support. Your plan for Thursday/Friday night is a little quick."

It appeared he was going to continue, but I really needed to emphasize a couple of points.

"Ted, I really appreciate your thoughts on using some extra time. But NO! I'm going forward and forcing Todd to be involved with me on this timetable. It starts tomorrow night trailing Don the Weasel, then Bethany and her yacht full of "johns". Then a confrontation in her office on Monday when they divide the "booty". I will not wait!"

I continued, "Be on board, help eliminate a drug ring that is operating under your nose or get out of the way!"

Todd was trying to hide a smile. He wanted to get this whole mess eliminated. Murder, drug running, prostitution, it needed to be eliminated. Lightmiller knew we had all the facts, and any threats of judicial territory was going to have no bearing with me – a civilian.

We outlined what we needed from him. It was decided that we would "cast the net" for tomorrow night drug run knowing it could be Friday night. We told Lightmiller what we thought, he added some valid points operationally for the ocean drug activity surveillance and we agreed.

Operation "Gotcha" as I called it was born.

Chapter 62

Winston was advised that Operation Gotcha was a go. He planned for the jet skis and checked my camera, night visions and hearing devices. Todd was going to supply his own equipment from the department. Susan would not act like she knew anything, as a precaution if someone in her office could be a mole.

It was about 7:00 pm when Todd and I made our way over to the Club. We decided to park further away and just wait for Don to show up.

Around 8:15 Don showed up. Todd began to record the events ever so softly. I was taking long range photos of Don from the time he got off his motorcycle, until he was in Henry's boat.

As usual, he pulled out slowly and left the dock area and slowly cruised into the ocean.

When we saw him starting to cruise, we ran for the jet skis and began to follow at a distance. All the time Todd was taking photos and recording the events.

And sure, as usual, it began. From out of the eastern sky, we saw some airplane running lights. Don turned his lights on and off just twice, then left them off.

Todd was in contact with Lightmiller telling him it was happening. Lightmiller acknowledged and would have his chase plane follow the aircraft– way after the drop took place.

The drop happened just as we hoped for. Plane came in low – lights off and was running parallel on the port side of Dons (really Henry's) boat. They dropped five large packages into the water. As soon as the packages hit the water, their mini blue lights activated.

Don was cruising and using a gaffing hook, pulled each one of them quickly into the boat. After the fifth package was retrieved, Don turned on all the lights on the boat, lit his pipe and cruised south to the dock area in Ft. Lauderdale.

We got it all between our two cameras. One third of Gotcha was on film. But Todd reminded me, all we had so far was a plane dropping off packages into the ocean and a man picking them up. No real evidence. For all we knew, it could be popcorn in those bundles. At least that was a good defense attorney would argue.

But there was more to come this night!

We followed at a distance as Don cruised into the warehouse dock area in F. Lauderdale. We stayed back while coming in from the ocean so as not to have us seen or heard since there were some bright lights entering the inlet from the ocean.

Again, like clockwork, the Drop began.

Don pulled up along the side of a dimly lit dock. He turned on his flashlight and focused into the warehouse area, then turned it off. About ten seconds went by before we say the truck pull up to the dock to meet Don.

Three "goons" got out, and we could see kept his hand close to his pistol. He began to throw up the five bundles to the men on the dock. After the fourth one – Stephanie pulled up in her Mercedes, got out and walked over to Don.

She threw him a large, padded envelope. We were assuming it was cash for the delivery. Then Stephanie yelled out to Don, "Hold on for a minute – I want to check this merchandise out!"

One of the men on the dock, opened a package, took some powder out, and mixed it with something. Waiting about 10 seconds, looked at the glass tube and then nodded an approval to Stephanie.

"Okay, go on", she yelled to Don.

Stephanie talked to the men in the truck, took what appeared to be some money and a small package (maybe drugs) from them and drove away.

Again, we got it all on recorded video and photos. But again, Todd reminded me," Matt, all we have is a video and photos of packaged delivery. We have no real evidence as to what's in those packages. Just remember how important it's going to be to get confessions from Stephanie."

We contacted Lightmiller. The plan was to let Stephanie go, but tail the truck with the drugs and find out where there were going. That was on Lightmiller, so we had to hope he and his people did not screw that up!

We followed Don back to the Club. Todd and I were filming and recording the events. Nothing too exciting on the way back. Except close to the clubs' dock, Todd dropped his cell phone and in reaching for it, revved up his jet ski. Crap! But seemed like Don did not hear it.

Don gassed up henrys boat, washed it down quickly and began to walk over to his motorcycle. Todd and I planned that Todd would jump off by the rock jetty with his camera and film Don.

Turned out, Don was a creature of habit. He sat on his motorcycle, opened the envelope Stephani gave him and counted his cash. All the while getting photographed by Lt. Todd Hahn.

Two thirds of the action plan was complete. Tomorrow night – maybe another drug run or the "john boat".

After Don left, Todd, and I both called Susan and Connie to let them know we were okay, and all went well. No problems at all. Obviously, they seemed relieved. I called Winston and told him the same good news and that I would be home soon.

"Very good sir, well done, see you soon," he said and hung up. A man of few words!

Todd headed towards home and I did the same thing. A shower was needed to get the salt spray off. I was asleep by 11:30.

Chapter 63

The next morning, Friday, I was awakened by Winston over the intercom telling me that Lt. Hahn and Agent Lightmiller were coming over mid-morning. I went downstairs to the kitchen and Winston was reading todays paper. Looking up – almost annoyed (what did I do?) he asked me.

"Coffee and danish sir?"

"Thanks Winston," I said.

I ran down the details of last night with him hoping for his approval. But what I got was the same lecture I got from Todd last night.

"Remember sir, all you have is pictures of airplanes in the night, dropping packages into the water. You have people throwing packages onto a dock and passing envelopes. And finally, a man on a motorcycle counting cash – all circumstantial. No real proof or evidence of anything."

Geez! Really? But I did understand. It would all have to come out when the confession came. And I was solely responsible for that. It was going to be on me and me alone to get everyone to talk – and not get shot doing it!

Todd and Lightmiller came over and we compared notes, photos, videos, and recordings. It all looked good on paper. But no real evidence that could be used in a court-yet!

Lightmiller said the DEA spotter team followed the plane back to Daytona beach. They had the serial number of the plane and were checking out its ownership. They would also put surveillance on the plane and see if it made a run somewhere else to pick up the drugs. Or if the drugs were delivered to them.

But we needed to continue our Plan.

It was Friday, and we knew it was going to be a big night on Bethany's Yacht. Birdie, her housekeeper told us, and we were going to follow that activity as well.

The thought of getting a judge to approve a listening device crossed our minds. But we decided against it. The less people knew about this – the better. Besides, we had the "johns" license plates and could easily locate them when the time came for corroboration.

Connie called later during the day and I shared with her that Todd and I were getting ready for tonight. I also reminded her that tonight was only a surveillance night. Photos only and not to worry.

As the day went on, we checked everything. No issues.

"Fresh batteries for the night visions and camera," piped Winston. "Leave nothing to chance," he said.

Todd and I drove over as a Team to the Yacht Brokerage Office. This is where the "johns" gathered and got on board for the night's activities.

Sure enough, as they came in, they parked their cars and walked over to the dock where Bethany's yacht was moored and, they all had briefcases with them.

"Gotcha!" And photographed!

Todd and I let them go. We would wait till they returned. Not sure how long that would be, we assumed 3 hours which was the time on the trips we recorded prior.

We were about to go get some dinner when my cell phone rang. It was Winston.

"Sir, if you'll look on your phone, I placed an application titled," Gotcha". It is a GPS application. I had a friend place a GPS Device on the underside of the swim deck back on the stern. You will be able to see where they go, but more importantly, when they return.

I would suggest NOT to tell Lt. Hahn." And with that Winston hung up.

Oh Baby, you gotta love this guy!

I told Todd lets go get some dinner. After a while, we finished dinner, walked a few docks admiring some of the sailboats moored in place. About 3 hours later, I "suggested" that we head back.

"Why now?" said Todd. "You know something about the return you are not sharing?"

"Actually yes. Let's just go and leave it at that for now." I spoke.

We went back, positioned ourselves and got some great photos of the men coming off. In addition, some additional photos of the "ladies" and Bethany.

We did notice one action event. One of the last men getting off the yacht seemed to pass a small package to one of the "ladies". He patted her on the butt and walked away.

But we saw that Bethany also saw that hand off activity as well. As the "lady" walked back on board, Bethany came down from the upper bridge deck. Grabbed her and slapped her with a huge left hand across her face. It knocked the young lady off balance and onto the deck.

"You don't take cash, jewelry or drugs from any of these guys – understand? Do it again and you'll find yourself with a pair of concrete heels and become nothing more than crab food! Understand?" Bethany roared.

The other four ladies came up after hearing the commotion. It was then that "lady luck" (sorry about that) shined on us.

Bethany assembled all the ladies and shouted out in rage,

" Understand this is my operation. You work for me and follow my rules. I control the purchase of the "johns", the money, the drug distribution with my daughter. Think these jerks love you? Think twice again. They love to give me their cash to launder, buy drugs, distribute them, and pay them back a nice profit. Take from me or my daughter Stephanie and it will be the end of you! Understand?"

"Operation Gotcha" just got this all on video, tape, and pictures. Now we were closer to real proof and real evidence.

Chapter 64

Todd was smiling all the way home. Not because we had any real overwhelming evidence, but he now knew this entire operation was real. And with a few more steps – the more difficult ones, a big ass case would close.

Todd called Susan and relayed information to her. I called Connie and relayed the same message and that we were both fine. All was well.

Winston was waiting on the front steps, smoking his pipe when I drove in. Like always, he starred at me and returned a cordial wave and a small head nod as I pulled in.

Sharing with Winston about the nights events and what we gathered was exciting because I knew I was closer to the final act of this play.

"Just remember sir, the most dangerous part of this has yet to occur," he said.

That night I slept well, knowing I had the beginnings of real evidence to put some people away. I still needed to tie in Don and or Bethany to the murder of Tobias and Brenda.

Not sure how I was going to do this. But it was not going to come to me tonight.

Saturday morning, I went into Todd's office and we met with Lightmiller. We showed him the video and especially the sound bite from Bethany.

Although not a real confession that would carry any real weight in a trial, he was impressed. It meant Lightmiller, Todd and I could start to put a real connection of the dots between Bethany, Don and Stephanie about the prostitution, drug running and money laundering and maybe murder.

Operation "Gotcha" was outlined by me and Todd to Lightmiller.

The plan was to have me loaded with a portable DVD player that was loaded with the video of the drug drops in the ocean to Don, the hand off by Don to Stephanie and her goons, Bethany and her "johns" and her outburst telling her ladies all about it. Drugs, sex money laundering and it was all under her control.

The final part of this charade was going to be in the Yacht Brokerage Office. It meant me and me alone had to get all the parties to "confess" – to everything.

 I was sure Don killed Tobias and Brenda. I suspected he would not think twice about killing me.

Bethany was also a hot head when provoked. I knew I could get under her skin.

Stephanie was the wild card in the group. Other than attending her wedding some months before and seeing her on the dock with her goons, she was the unknown to me.

Lightmiller, Todd, backup and the technicians would be nearby listening. When they got what they all needed, they would come in hot and heavy. I added that I wanted to add the verb – fast – as well.

They repeatedly asked if I could pull this off. "Yes, I know just what to say and do to irritate them to a point of confession before they want to either take me out or try to bring me into the operation. Don't worry I have it all planned out," I said.

Truth be told, I was going to need Sunday to think this through.

We loaded my portable video player. It was all I needed for the final part of "Gotcha"

It was now up to me to bring this to a close Monday morning.

Chapter 65

Sunday was going to be a planning day. But I know Connie would want to do something during the day. Todd and I both agreed we would not tell the girls it was going down on Monday morning. They'd just worry.

My plan was to meet with Connie, go for a drive and sometime on the beach. Then back to my place, jump into the pool, then shower, have dinner and take her home. That would give me time to finalize my plans for tomorrow.

Fortunately for me, Connie called about 8:30 in the morning.

"Matt, I know we were going to do something today, but I have three emergencies, "she said.

"Two dogs hit by cars that are going to require some surgery and a seeing eye dog with some allergies I need to treat."

"How about tomorrow night after work," she asked.

"Great honey, no problem, take care of our canine friends. Talk to you later tonight," I replied.

Okay, that takes of that problem, (kind of as I do love being with her).

So, my rehearsal began for tomorrow. I was trying to time when I thought confessions would come forward. Also, if they would know that I, "got them" and would invite me into the operation.

The other thought that was lingering that I tried to push away, the thought of them just shooting me in the office and taking my body out to sea.

After two hours of rehearsing, I decide to take a swim. I needed to clear my head and think it through – underwater.

Winston had dinner for me, and I shared my plan in detail with him. Even shared with him the office layout, the two entrances to the brokerage office (front door and side door), the furniture placement, and windows. If this whole thing went south, I had a plan to jump behind the couch while being shot at or jump out the window before returning fire.

He simply nodded, stroked his beard, and said, "Sounds acceptable – good luck sir," and walked away.

A few minutes later he walked into the kitchen with my 9mm.

"Sir, I cleaned it, loaded it and have two extra clips for you, should you need them."

"Winston, thank you. Hopefully, I won't need them and Todd, Lightmiller and backup will come is like the calvary," I said.

"Yes sir," said Winston and walked away.

Chapter 66

It was Monday morning. Got up about 5:30 and started thinking about today's events.

Had some coffee and some cereal but I wasn't hungry.

Called Connie and asked how her day went yesterday. She had sent me a text last night before she went to bed. But I thought I would talk to her, one more time today.

I called Todd around 9:00 and he told me his team was in place watching for any activity at Bethany's office. He was coming over now with the wire and a technician to test it out. Already, I had made the decision to allow them to wire me but was going to take it off and use my cell phone – live to Todd.

When they came by, I surprised the listening device it was going to be an exceedingly small that clipped to the back under my collar. And a with a very thin wire that ran from the back of my shirt, under the collar to the front with a small, attached microphone.

It would allow me to raise up my shirt from the waist up, turn around and show them no wires. I had to be fast as I was going to set down my live cell on a nearby table as well as hold the video player.

No sooner had we attached the wire to me when Todd got the call.

Bethany and Stephanie had arrived, so we knew Don would be close behind.

Chapter 67

We jumped into Todd's Crown Vic and sped down to the yacht brokerage office. Lights but no sirens allowed us to make great time. We got about two blocks away when we turned off the lights. His team had just reported Don had arrived and was also inside.

They also reported that the secretary came out the front door, got in her car and was driving away.

I started to get out of his car when he grabbed my arm, "Matt don't try to be a hero. If it is not going to happen – walk away. There is always another day, another opportunity. We will all be downstairs, but you are own your own until we get there if something goes wrong– understand?"

"Actually Todd, today needs to be the day to end this, once and for all. If nothing else and it goes wrong, you can always get them for my murder." Gosh, did I just say that?

"Lightmiller – do not screw this up," I jokingly told him as I walked towards the office.

Video player, check. Cell phone turned on and connected to Todd's, check. My two cousins also came, Smith & Wesson, check.

I walked up the stairs, down the short breezeway and opened the door to the brokerage office.

Chapter 68

When I walked into the office door, Bethany was behind her desk, Stephanie was standing next to her and Don was sitting in front of her desk. So far so good.

Knowing there was only one way to do this, I started.

"Hey, look, it's my favorite band of murderers, drug runners and prostitution madams."

With that, Don the Weasel jumped up out of his chair and made a move towards me. I was mentally prepared for his move, but Bethany yelled out to him.

"Don, stop, now, "she said as she stood up behind her desk.

"What the hell are you talking about you worthless piece of shit," Don stated.

Before I could let anything else be said, I placed the small video player on the table in front of Bethany's desk. I had it set for a series of video clips on a loop.

 One was Don in the boat at night, the next was him passing drugs on the dock to Stephanie and the third was video of Bethany, her "johns" and her girls.

What happened next was not expected.

Stephanie reached into her purse, pulled out a small pistol and fired almost point blank at me, all the time yelling, "You're not going to ruin us." Fortunately, the shot missed and went wide left. That happens quite a bit with inexperienced people shooting pistols in a rage. Using their index finger, they pull too hard – too fast and the shots go left – if you're right-handed. Lucky for me!

"Stephanie, stop it," yelled Bethany. "Not here, not now," as Bethany reached for her pistol.

I needed to reply quickly so Todd and the gang who would hear the shot – not come up yet.

"Nice shot, hope your better at your drug running business than you are shot," I said somewhat nervously.

Don was fixated on the video. He now saw he had been tracked, trailed, and recorded. He knew the video made it clear it was him.

"Don." I began. "I've got you using a club members boat that you sold him – Henry. I've also got you recorded on three drug running operations picking up the drops in the ocean and bringing them to Stephanie."

"Stephanie – take a close look," I started with. "I've got you on a number of drug smuggling runs, taking the packages from Don. See how pretty you look on a telephoto lens? The DEA is goanna love this video."

I continued towards Bethany, "Bethany, I've got you on numerous prostitutions, drug distribution and money laundering – look at the video. Its only one of a number that I have been recording."

About that time, Don reached into his briefcase and pulled out what looked like a Bursa 9m and he was attaching a silencer on the end of the barrel. This was not good.

"Hey Weasel, you are not going to shoot me in this office. No way to get me out of here and not have someone see you taking a body out – right Bethany?" "And besides dumb shit – you have no idea what I have done with the original versions – much longer in length."

"Put the piece away," Bethany said to Don. I was still a little worried as Stephanie's gun was still on the table – not knowing who may pick it up.

I figured at this point I needed to play to Don being emotional, irrational, and stupid.

Going out on a limb, "So Don why kill Brenda the waitress at the club?"
Before Bethany could stop him, Don replied," because the ol bitty came out and saw me and Tobias one night and wondered what we

were doing. So, I told Bethany and we agreed to kill her. No loose ends."

"Who else has this?", yelled Stephanie.

"Stephanie, I only look stupid – maybe a lot of people – maybe no one," I replied as I turned towards Bethany.

"Bethany, as a trust funder, why more? Why drugs and prostitution? And poor Tobias" I asked.

"Poor Tobias my ass," Bethany replied. "When he heard we were making tons of money on the drugs, little Mr. Boy scout was upset when he found out his salesman Don and his daughter, Stephanie had a great thing going. Sure, he was okay with prostitution, but no drugs."

Again, I directed my question, looking at Don and Bethany for what I hoped was the obvious,

" So, Tobias objected to the money laundering and drugs, so you had killed him?"

Remember, I saw Don on his motorcycle and saw him the night he killed Tobias.

Don popped up with," no you little jerk, me and Bethany talked about it and we agreed. I killed him. Freed us up to do more, earn more, be more!"

"Mother", cried Stephanie, "You told me dad was killed by an unknown assailant! You and Don killed dad?"

Emotions were getting a little raw, so I decided to quickly try to scale it down.

"Who do you think got you into this little business enterprise? You sure seem to love the money and everything it does for you? House, cars, clothes jewelry. Sorry Stephanie, we needed your dad out of the way," she blurted out.

"I cannot believe you and Don killed dad," Stephanie said.

"Who do you think got you into the drug distribution business? asked Bethany.

She continued," we needed more money to grow – so we got our "johns" involved. They fronted cash, we bought the drugs, Don did the pickups at night, brought them to you and then you distributed them. And we gave back the "johns" a nice return on their money."

The next few moments are a blur.

Stephanie was pissed, she grabbed the gun on the table and shot Don, hitting him in his left arm.

Don grabbed his gun and was pointing it at Stephanie, when Bethany pulled out her piece from the desk drawer, pointed it at Don and said, "NO".

About that time, Todd and Lightmiller heard all they needed and came barging in the front door.

Don turned and fired at Todd. Todd sensed it and moved to the right and went to take cover behind the sofa. Don fired again, hitting Todd in the chest and then he fired another round at Lightmiller - who went down.

Todd fired back and hit Don in the leg, and he went down in agony.

Meanwhile Bethany has me dead in her sights with her 9mm.

I saw her pointing her gun right at me, finger on the trigger and yelling – "I swear I'm going to kill you!"

The next thing I heard was a sound like a cannon going off and seeing Bethany's body flying over the desk while the back of her head was being plastered against the wall.

Looking up from the floor I saw Winston. He had come in the office from the back door in the hallway and took Bethany out with his .50 caliber. The explosion, smoke and ear piercing sound from his gun was a comfort to me.

Stephanie froze and fell to the floor sobbing, "daddy, I'm so sorry.".

It was over.

Chapter 69

The wrap up.

Todd and Lightmiller were both wearing bullet proof vest that day. So, they only suffered a couple of broken ribs and the embarrassment that Don got the drop on them.

Don the Weasel, admitted to killing Brenda and Tobias. He was truly afraid of his future in prison and tried to make a deal. But while he thought he was smart – in fact, he was an errand boy for Bethany and Stephanie. He described the schedule of picking up the drugs and gave all the details to Lightmiller. He was going to stand trial for two first degree murders, attempted killing of a police detective and a federal agent, plus numerous other crimes involving drugs. Don was going away for a long time.

Bethany was dead. But her ledgers were in her desk, so it was going to be easy for Todd and Lightmiller to pick up the Johns and get more information from all of them. Besides, we had them on video and long-range photos. They easily talked to make a deal.

Stephanie confessed to a drug distribution deal. She never mentioned another club member. But one thing I barely saw on one of the photos was "Fillstrom Trucking" nearby. I was sure Rodney Fillstrom may have been involved. I saved this little piece of information for myself and decided I would investigate Rodney Fillstrom later.

Stephanie was also going away for a long time. Side note, Stephanie's new husband was totally in the dark about her illegal activities. He divorced her quietly and moved to Maine.

And while I felt a bit sad for Tobias, I could not understand that with all the money and prestige, was how come they all wanted more – by any means. Country Club Greed.

I did go over to Brenda's grave and place a nice bouquet of flowers on her headstone. As I stood there thinking what a waste. All this hatred, murder and cheating for more money. How much is enough?

As I starred at Brenda's headstone all I could say was...

"Brenda, I got him for you. Rest in peace."

And what about Winston and his involvement.

Well, let's just say that both Todd and Lightmiller put it into their report that Winston was a key member of this take down team.

Rodney – you spoiled brat. You took over your dads trucking business and you're doing bad stuff.

I am coming for you.

Country Club – Trucking

Rodney Fillstrom was a 43-year-old spoiled brat. His father died filling in of one of his drivers delivering a load to Atlanta.

Rodney – who has a Commercial Drivers License ended up taking over his dad's firm. Although Rodney never drove, he always acted like a big punk.

But when one of his trucks is spotted in the immediate area of a drug distribution sting, Matt Tucker stays quiet.

Matt starts looking into Rodney, his gambling activity at the Atlantic Country Club where he is a member. And what Matt finds is a series of crimes that involve murder, drugs, and human trafficking.

All for more cash.

Country Club Greed – Trafficking.

But when Matt and Connie gets too close – things take a turn putting Matt in the crosshairs of a diabolical scheme for prostitution and what appears to be a human trafficking labor scheme.

Moving drugs in tankers, moving people in refrigerated vans for forced labor in South Florida.

You'll want to follow Matt and Connie as they uncover this plot – but not before they find themselves victims. Can Lt. Hahn help? Can Winston locate them and save their lives.

The action continues with Stockers next action pack thriller "Country Club Greed-Trafficking.